DERBYSHIRE

Detail & Character

A Celebration of its Towns & Villages

Consult the Genius of the Place in all

Alexander Pope

God is in the details

Mies Van Der Rohe (attributed)

DERBYSHIRE

Detail & Character

A Celebration of its Towns & Villages

Barry Joyce

PHOTOGRAPHS BY
Gordon Michell
& Mike Williams

FOREWORD BY
JONATHAN DIMBLEBY

SUTTON PUBLISHING

First published in the United Kingdom in 1996 by
Alan Sutton Publishing Ltd , an imprint of Sutton Publishing Limited
Phoenix Mill · Thrupp · Stroud · Gloucestershire GL5 2BU
in association with Derbyshire County Council

Reprinted 1999

A catalogue record for this book is available from the British Library.

ISBN 0-7509-0737-1

Half-title page: Top left: Stacked timber spouting, Chesterfield. Bottom left: Moulded brick
letter, Ilkeston. Top right: Numeral plaque, Wirksworth. Bottom right: Setts and cobbles,
Ashbourne. *Frontispiece:* The Churchyard of St Edmund in Castleton with Mam Tor looming
beyond the roofs of the houses and shops which line the village street.
Cover photographs: Front, Long Row, Belper. Back, view from the tower of St Mary's church,
Wirksworth, looking towards West End.

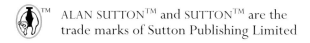 ALAN SUTTON™ and SUTTON™ are the
trade marks of Sutton Publishing Limited

Typeset in 12/17 Perpetua
Typesetting and origination by
Sutton Publishing Limited.
Printed in Great Britain by
Butler & Tanner, Frome, Somerset.

CONTENTS

A new cutlery factory on the outskirts of Hathersage (see p. 75). This was designed by architect Michael Hopkins for David Mellor, designer and manufacturer.

FOREWORD

There is no greater environmental challenge as we approach the end of the millennium than to arrest the pervasive ubiquity that now threatens England's towns and villages. Our land is renowned for its remarkable diversity – from the harsh granite moors of Cornwall and Devon to the soft lush valleys of the Yorkshire and Derbyshire Dales – and buildings make an important contribution to this diversity and sense of place. Yet pressures for development – from out of town shopping centres and housing estates, to roadside kerbing, sign posts and paving – are posing an increasing threat to local distinctiveness. As with our language, we are in danger of losing touch with the rich variety of 'dialects' of local building styles and materials.

I am pleased, therefore, to commend to you this important book, which identifies and celebrates the diversity and distinctiveness to be found in the buildings of Derbyshire. This subject is approached with great sensitivity and understanding, which I hope will inspire active appreciation and protection of the county's built environment. More than this, the book should be used as a guide by all those who build in Derbyshire to help them to enhance rather than dilute the spirit of this beautiful county. Its messages must be translated from the page to real decisions about new development in the county. I also hope that other local authorities will follow the example set by Derbyshire County Council in producing this book.

It is vital that in striving for a better understanding of our built heritage and associated traditional building skills we do not become blind to the need for good contemporary design. Understanding and respect for past building traditions should inform rather than restrict the application of new technologies. We should seek to create a distinctive set of buildings of this age of which we can be proud.

The quality of new development in the countryside has been an abiding concern of the Council for the Protection of Rural England, of which I am President, since its establishment 70 years ago. This concern was best expressed perhaps by the architect Clough Williams-Ellis, an early CPRE activist, who wrote:

Almost any traditional regional flavouring is now well worth preserving for the sake of variety in a world gone sadly flat. It should be a matter of pride as well as of good sense, good economics and good manners, for everyone to see to it that new works of whatever kind shall express themselves politely in accents that are recognisably regional and not harshly alien to an ancient and honourable tradition.

This book should give you a taste of the regional flavours to be found in just one English county. It demonstrates that in Derbyshire there is still a lot to safeguard and cherish.

JONATHAN DIMBLEBY
President
Council for the Protection of Rural England

From the top of Farhill the village of Ashover lies in the Amber Valley, concealed by trees. Only the 128 foot high spire of the parish church of All Saints rises above their canopy.

INTRODUCTION

This book is a celebration of local character in the towns and villages of Derbyshire.

CHARACTER

What is local character? What makes a place *distinctive* – different from anywhere else?

There are many contributory factors. Landscape, language, occupations, customs, food, buildings and spaces between buildings are some of them. Combined, they determine the particular identity of a place – the characteristics which become familiar and give people a sense of *belonging*.

We can no longer take the richness and diversity of different localities for granted. Modern ways of life are leading to much greater uniformity. A motorway service station in Nottinghamshire may be indistinguishable from one in Kent, or even Calais. Bread baked to a standard formula, cut to standard slices and sold in standard wrapping will taste and look the same no matter in which of fifty locations it has been produced.

Buildings and paving, and the materials from which they are made, are major factors which determine the distinctiveness of our towns and villages. For centuries, limitations in transport meant that, for purely economic reasons, buildings were constructed from the ground beneath them – either stone straight from local quarries or brick baked from local clay, with roofs covered with local straw, reed or heather, or with thin slabs of local stone or tiles made of local baked clay.

The materials automatically look right for a particular place because they come from that place. The colour is right, the texture is right and even the shapes determined by the materials are right.

The character of the buildings is further enhanced and made more distinctive by the local tradition in building craftsmanship. For example, it is only in Derbyshire and Yorkshire that eaves gutters are (still) commonly made from a solid balk of timber. Further regional diversity comes from the dialect terms[1] used for such gutters – LAUNDERS in the Matlock area, SPOUTING in the Chesterfield area and TROWS around New Mills and Glossop.

This book attempts to reveal some of this rich patchwork of distinctiveness in the county of Derbyshire. Of course, the economic discipline which determined the use of local building materials and local craftsmanship is now no more, but to some extent it still happens – through choice.

---

1 A list of Derbyshire dialect building terms is given on p. 137.

That choice may be personal — made by the individual — or collective — as expressed through the town and country planning system. However, it has to be said that what was once the cheapest and most convenient way of building is now only followed by deliberate choice and often at greater cost.

To what extent then are we indulging in nostalgia? It is alleged by some that we have an obsession with the past and that this is an indication of national decline and stagnation. Some claim that our system of protecting historic buildings is too restrictive. Nevertheless, our built 'heritage' is a finite thing — once it has gone it cannot be recreated — and it is widely prized and enjoyed.

There need be no battle between conservation and creativity. It is not a matter of having one or the other. Without creativity and innovation, conservation becomes a sterile dead-end. The challenge is to marry the two. By keeping and adapting our old buildings for new uses, we are not only preserving our heritage but acting on the sound 'green' principle of avoiding waste. The earth summit at Rio de Janeiro in 1992 identified *sustainability* as a key environmental issue. It is a rather abstract concept, but in the context of urban conservation the cost of using traditional local materials and workmanship may be set against the cost of long-distance transport and the use of artificial materials which require high-energy production methods.

Following the same principle, where new buildings are needed they should, wherever possible, be on derelict sites within the urban framework, thereby minimizing the need for travel, preserving open countryside and improving the urban scene. Where this is done it is important for the designer to have an understanding of the urban context and its particular character.

DETAIL

By focusing on *detail*, the component parts of a building or street scene can be analysed and more easily understood and enjoyed. The images speak for themselves. The humble, even commonplace, detail which is shown to contribute to an area's distinctive character is likely to be more widely valued and cared for as a result.

The selected images include many elements in the local scene which have no formal protection, the preservation of which lies essentially in the hands of the owners. No matter how comprehensive any imposed system of protection may be, it cannot be effective if the majority of people who own and use the buildings and places are not, themselves, in sympathy with the need for preservation.

The pity is that while there is very considerable sympathy for, and commitment to, conservation, the small details which add up to make the bigger picture of the country village, the industrial hamlet or the market town are rarely valued in their own right. How many paid-up members of the National Trust come back from a visit to a country house to their own homes where sash windows have been replaced with brown-stained casements with stick-on leaded lights — all done with the best possible intentions? The grand façade of the country house may be admired for its handsomely proportioned windows, but what of the brilliance of the old crown glass in the Yorkshire sashes of the cottage next door? Are those windows not also worthy of our attention and care?

If such apparently unremarkable elements of the traditional scene are to be preserved, it is incumbent on those of us who feel strongly about it to explain *why* they have significance.

This book is not, however, solely concerned with preservation. It is also intended to be of use to architects and builders as a reference to assist in the process of the design and construction of new buildings. The cutlery factory at Hathersage (pp. 6 and 75) is an excellent example of how knowledge of local building materials and traditional construction details has been fundamental to the development of a building that speaks of its own time and yet fits so well into the local scene.

Analysis of detail is also valuable for the teacher. Through a study of it, evidence of past ways of life, economic conditions, changing patterns of transport and attitudes to social issues may all be teased out of the places in which we live.

A school trip to the 'plague' village of Eyam may be a valuable way to learn about social conditions in the seventeenth century, but there is no need to travel far from the school gates to investigate the past. Every area has its own history, in stone or brick, or plaster or slate, if the knowledge is there to interpret it.

DERBYSHIRE – THE RAW MATERIALS

Derbyshire is a county of outstanding natural beauty. Twenty million people a year seek out its hills and dales. It is also a county of stone and minerals. From beneath the surface of its landscape the riches and complexity of its geology have provided its people, over the centuries, with durable and handsome building materials on their doorstep. It has also yielded the raw materials for energy and manufacturing – albeit much of it needing to be hard won.

At the conclusion of the twentieth century we see the end of the county's coal-mining industry. The previous century saw the end of the county's ancient lead-mining industry. A surveyor in 1811 listed 500 collieries and 300 lead or other mineral mines. Their names read like poetry and summon up a vivid picture of the life of the miners and their quest into the bowels of the earth: Bage, Ball-eye, Blobber, Cackle-Mackle, Carrion-hole, Dimple, Fiery Dragon, Golconda, Hell Rake, Jowl-groove, Meerbrook, Mockshaw, Nestus, Odin, Perseverance, Raddle-pits, Raven Tor, Sallet-hole, Suckstone, Thistley, Venture, Virgin, Warm-bath, Wig-twizzle, Yoke-cliffe.

In addition to lead, iron and coal, Derbyshire's rocks yielded up alabaster, barytes, bloodstone, Blue-John, calcedony, dog-tooth spar, fluor-spar, gypsum, jasper, lapis calaminaris, marl, ochre, pyrites, sulphur, toadstone and zinc – a veritable cornucopia of minerals, some of which were used to decorate and embellish the buildings and gardens of the county.

Less exotic but equally rich is the range of Derbyshire's basic building materials. The dark pink/grey/brown Millstone Grit runs diagonally from Glossop to Derby and rises north of Bakewell to make the Dark Peak. West of this lies the hard, light-grey, fossil-rich, Carboniferous Limestone of the White Peak, and east of it the soft, sandy, brown Coal Measures sandstone of the Nottinghamshire–Derbyshire coalfield. Derbyshire juts out east of that, around Bolsover, to take in part of the band of creamy white Magnesian Limestone which outcrops just north of Nottingham and runs into the sea at Tyneside.

In the south of the county, below Ashbourne and Derby, where stone was far less readily available, early builders utilized timber much more because it was relatively plentiful. Later, the clays of lowland Derbyshire came to be widely used for the making of brick. But even in the clay lowlands, nowhere was more than 10 miles from a sandstone or gritstone outcrop which could be quarried.

Then there are the eccentric diversions to this main theme, such as the streaky bacon coloured alabaster which occurs at Chellaston and which gives the suburban rockeries of south Derby such a distinctive appearance.

However, this is not an attempt at a comprehensive or academic analysis of Derbyshire's building materials – although such a volume would be welcome; rather it is a series of selective images to give a taste of what lies there, ready to be enjoyed.

Twenty-five or so towns and villages have been put under the microscope, as it were, selected to represent the different parts of the county, from the uplands of the Dark Peak of the north-west, to the White Peak in the west, the Derwent Valley running down the centre, and the coalfield of the eastern side to the lowlands of the Erewash Valley, the Trent Valley and beyond.

Between these sub-regions there is a considerable range of building materials, detail, character and way of life, and yet to its people Derbyshire has meaning as an entity, as was revealed in the recent review of local government. It is also of considerable age as an administrative area, having emerged as a result of a reorganization of local government by the Anglo-Saxon kings in the tenth century. Its boundaries survive much as they were created over a millennium ago. On the eve of a new millennium it is appropriate to celebrate the special character of Derbyshire's towns and villages.

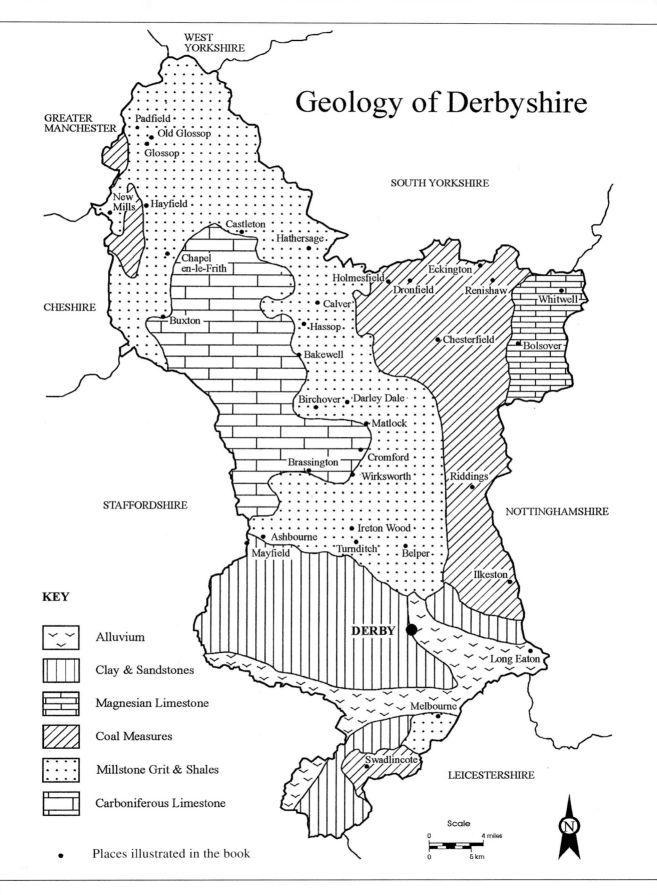

Geology of Derbyshire

WEST YORKSHIRE

GREATER MANCHESTER

SOUTH YORKSHIRE

CHESHIRE

STAFFORDSHIRE

NOTTINGHAMSHIRE

LEICESTERSHIRE

Padfield
Old Glossop
Glossop
New Mills
Hayfield
Castleton
Hathersage
Chapel en-le-Frith
Holmesfield
Eckington
Dronfield
Renishaw
Whitwell
Calver
Buxton
Hassop
Chesterfield
Bolsover
Bakewell
Birchover
Darley Dale
Matlock
Cromford
Brassington
Wirksworth
Riddings
Ireton Wood
Ashbourne
Turnditch
Belper
Mayfield
Ilkeston
DERBY
Long Eaton
Melbourne
Swadlincote

KEY

∨∨∨	Alluvium
|||||	Clay & Sandstones
▤	Magnesian Limestone
▨	Coal Measures
⋯	Millstone Grit & Shales
▦	Carboniferous Limestone
•	Places illustrated in the book

Scale
0   4 miles
0   5 km

N

BUILDING CRAFTS

If new buildings are to fit harmoniously into the cherished local scene and if old buildings are to be lovingly repaired for the use and enjoyment of future generations, there is one absolute requirement: the continuation of traditional building crafts.

These crafts deserve celebration in their own right. We owe a great debt to the people who carry the knowledge and skill from one generation to another.

In the past, economics was the prime motivating force, but now very often those engaged in traditional building crafts battle against market forces, their motivation coming from the satisfaction gained from exercising their skills and talents.

Some skills have been lost altogether. While there are still a few roofers expert in the craft of laying sandstone roof 'slates', there are no stone slate makers in Derbyshire, the last ones having finally abandoned their uneconomic trade in the 1950s. If stone slate roofs are to remain one of the glories of Derbyshire's built heritage, new sources of stone roofing slates have to be found. The process of stripping roofs to provide material for repairing others can only last so long.

It is encouraging that the ancient craft of making lime putty (mortar) is gaining in vigour (see pp. 20 and 21). It suggests that the period when traditional building crafts were abandoned for the brave new world is over and that the merits of age-old traditions and practices are being rediscovered. Let us hope so.

Files, shears, hacksaws, cold chisels, welding goggles, punches and other tools of blacksmith Simon Vaughan in his smithy at Wirksworth.

Derbyshire is above all a county of stone. It has been a source of good building stone ever since buildings were first erected. When the old Houses of Parliament were destroyed by fire in 1834 a commission was set up to scour the kingdom for the best possible stone for the replacement building. In 1839 it eventually reported its findings and Magnesian Limestone from Bolsover was the first choice: 'For advantage of colour the Magnesian Limestone, or dolomite, of Bolsover Moor and its neighbourhood is in our opinion the most fit and proper material to be employed in the proposed new Houses of Parliament.' The gritstone of Darley Dale was also praised. This pinky-buff coarse-grained sandstone is the main building stone for central Derbyshire, used for cottage and palace alike. In 1994 it was chosen by architect Michael Hopkins for his new annexe to the Houses of Parliament. These massive blocks in the Anne Twyford Quarry at Birchover, near Matlock, are the first step in the production of fine ashlar masonry, ultimately to be seen gracing the streetscape of Westminster.

Gritstone is also known as Millstone Grit since, as its secondary name suggests, as well as being a building stone it was sought out to produce grindstones and millstones, because of its great durability. Part-fashioned circular grindstones can be found in long-abandoned quarries, such as one at Alderwasley, which was in operation in 1257. Although only few building stone quarries operate today, for hundreds of years most towns and villages had their own quarry, or quarries, on their doorstep.

A level building site is rare in Derbyshire and advantage was sometimes taken of old quarry beds, on hillsides, to provide level platforms on which to build. In these cases the quarry is literally the doorstep.

At Babington House (on p. 37) geologists have been able to identify the correlation between each course of the Carboniferous Limestone walls with the strata of the 40 foot quarry face, from which the stone was won, just yards away in the back garden. The extent of the use of stone today is limited, essentially, by cost. Rubble stonework, that is stones which have not been given a finished face, is about twice as expensive as brickwork. Squared and dressed stonework is about three times as expensive. However, the investment is generally repaid through increased market value.

Building stone is still won, as it has been for hundreds of years, by drilling, blasting with black powder (gunpowder) and then splitting by the hammering of a 'plug' (chisel) between two 'feathers' (metal wedges). Here they are seen at the Anne Twyford Quarry, Birchover, as the quarryman has just left them, when he broke off for his snap (lunch).

The quarry is a much safer place than it once was. Horrific tales are told of injuries caused by careless use of gunpowder — of men impaled with iron bars which shot out like javelins when they were tamping the black powder into drilled holes. Men still living describe how they witnessed their grandfathers make fuses by filling corn straws with gunpowder — often done at home on the living-room table.

All over the limestone part of the county can be found the remains of small lime-kilns, where stone was dug locally and burned, mainly for use on the fields but also to make mortar and plaster. The Lime-Kiln is a common pub name. The small field kilns operate no more, but in the Buxton area massive industrial kilns produce large quantities of burnt lime and some of it is still used for making mortar.

Lime putty has been the basic ingredient of mortar and plaster since antiquity. Vitruvius, the Roman authority on architecture and building, recommended that it should be left a minimum of 10 years to mature before it was used for fine work.

The invention of Portland cement in 1824 led to the gradual decline and virtual extinction of the building lime putty mortar tradition by the 1930s. It is now, gradually, being used again because its unique qualities are once more being recognized and valued — especially for historic buildings. Here (opposite), burnt Carboniferous Limestone from Buxton, reduced to powder, is being mixed with water to form lime putty.

The haze is not dust but steam. Cold water mixed with the burnt lime quickly reaches boiling point as a result of a chemical reaction. Hard rock is transformed into soft putty. It is then run into plastic tubs for despatch all over the country and beyond. Derbyshire is by far the principal source of burnt lime in the United Kingdom. The plant of Bleaklow Industries at Hassop near Bakewell is the largest of its type.

Above Stacked half-round copings for the top of a wall ready for delivery.

The massive blocks won from the ground by the quarryman need to be converted to usable sizes: smaller blocks for coursed walling, slabs for paving or pieces for carving into architectural detail. The detailed work is done by 'banker masons', so called because they work at a banker – a mason's bench.

A mason must know the direction of the grain of a block of stone, much as a joiner does with wood. All sedimentary stones, laid down on a river or seabed, are made up of very thin layers, one on top of the other. If a stone is 'face-bedded', that is laid with the layers facing outwards, it will be prone to decay. Frost action can peel off the face layer of stone when it is wet. It is therefore important for stones to be laid with their natural bed horizontal.

The banker mason can give stone a number of surface finishes, such as hammer dressed, boasted, furrowed or finely tooled, depending on the style required. These finishes give life to the material, catching light on the raised parts and casting shadows in the grooves. See the tooled pattern to the door surround on p. 36. A beautifully tooled surface makes the most of a magnificent material. The work calls for great skill.

Opposite A ball finial is here being finished off by Carl Wragg at the workshop of Heritage Masonry at Whittington near Chesterfield. Carl was a banker mason for 15 years at the Anne Twyford Quarry, Birchover, following in the steps of his father, who had worked as a mason at the quarry for more than 50 years.

A salvaged sandstone roof slate being 'dressed' to a new size by John Thompson of H. & W. Sellors Ltd, masons and stone slate roofers of Bakewell. The Sellors family are virtually hereditary masons to the Dukes of Devonshire. See p. 33 for an example of their work.

Stone slates have a long history of use in Derbyshire. Diamond-shaped stone slates were found, in 1980, in an archaeological dig at the site of a second to fourth century Romano-British dwelling, now under the water of Carsington Reservoir. The family name Stonethacker was known in Chesterfield during the fourteenth and fifteenth centuries.

Salvaged slates stacked in Sellors' yard. These are sorted to size using a slater's rule or 'wippet stick', as it is known in the north of England. The rule is marked off in a series of gradations, three inches separating one size from another, with names such as 'batchelors', 'becks', 'sketchens' and 'fairwells' given to the main sizes.

The burgeoning of DIY stores and the double-glazing industry has contributed to the disappearance of many small joiners versed in traditional skills and with knowledge of local door and window patterns. Happily, some survive, and there may even be a modest resurgence as a result of a growing commitment to conservation.

J. N. Cocker, purpose-made joinery specialists based in Buxton, have developed out of a building contractor's business founded by John Cocker's uncle. On the death of his uncle in the mid-1970s, John, who had originally been apprenticed to his father who also worked in the business, took it over and began to specialize in good quality joinery. Now his son, Steve, works with him, but also has his own joinery business. They work from a small, immaculately kept workshop, the confined quarters of which must have presented a major problem when they won the contract to remake the stage in the refurbishment of Frank Matcham's Buxton Opera House.

This gate, at the entrance to Potter's Yard, Melbourne, was made in 1991 for new owners who brought this pleasant little backwater back to life by renovating the buildings and finding new uses for them.

Opposite   The appropriately named Bill Smith began to learn his trade at the age of 15, when he became an apprentice at the Derby railway works, following in the steps of his father and grandfather. In 1987 he took over the smithy at Church Street, Melbourne, becoming the successor to numerous craftsmen who worked the same forge for more than 200 years. The date 1795 is burnt into the timber bressummer (beam) that supports the forge hood.

Having been for most of his working life involved with industrial forging and blacksmithying, he now carries out the role of a village smith, making spout brackets, door latches, gates, railings and anything else that is called for.

The roofscape of St Mary's Gate and St John Street, Wirksworth, viewed from the tower of the medieval parish church of St Mary. The close proximity of one building to another probably stems from a pattern of building established in the Middle Ages.

ROOFS
AND WALLS

The roofs and walls of traditional buildings make up the big blocks of colour and texture which set the scene in towns and villages. They give the clue to the geology of the ground beneath and, where they are directly related to that geology, they are in complete visual harmony with the landscape in which they sit. However, improvements in transport in the eighteenth and nineteenth centuries brought about variations to that set pattern. Therefore the range of types and colours of roofs throughout the county is a product of only the past couple of hundred years or so.

Local clays in places like Ashbourne and Melbourne enabled the Georgians to make red clay tiles, but by the 1720s the fiery orange red pantile was finding its way into the county and with the coming of canals and railways the dark blue clay tiles of Staffordshire and the grey and green slates of Wales and Cumbria were being used in quantity. Before then the vast majority of cottages and houses were roofed in thatch.

The handful of thatched roofs which can be seen now give no idea of what Derbyshire thatch looked like. Unlike today's covering of neatly manicured reed, imported from East Anglia, they were laid with bundles of long straw from the fields and, surprisingly, finished along their ridges and verges with mud, giving a wonderfully soft and rounded outline, rather like a tea cosy.

Churches and the very grandest houses, like Haddon Hall, were often roofed in lead, sometimes from the patron's or owner's own mines, but the middling houses were, and largely still are, crowned with the most handsome covering of all, Derbyshire stone slate, a material that, like lead, was valued in Roman times.

Some of the earliest walling in Derbyshire is timber-framing, albeit much of it now hidden behind later skins of stone or brick. The very earliest is made up of half trees shaped into curved members called crucks, put together to form a simple A-shaped frame. But there is nowhere in the county far from a source of good walling stone and it is its stone buildings which are the county's glory.

Sometimes the living rock is used as the base of a wall, the wrought stone rising from it almost imperceptibly. To the sheer beauty of its natural colour is added the contribution of the mason in the form of intricate surface patterns and finishes. Further interest is given through architectural detail. Gables may be capped with shaped coping stones and sometimes crowned with decorative finials. The corners of walls are given structural and visual strength by the use of large quoins, alternating between long and short. Door and window openings are spanned with lintels, either plain rectangles or wedge-shaped, and window openings are sometimes subdivided with stone mullions, older houses having shaped ones and later windows square-faced ones.

Brick buildings have their own distinctive details. In the same way that the character of a stone wall is determined by the depth of each course, its colour and the surface pattern given it by the mason, the character of a brick wall is determined by the pattern of bonding (the way the bricks are arranged). Early brickwork is generally English bond – alternating layers of all headers (bricks laid with their ends to the wall face) and all stretchers (bricks laid with their sides to the face). In the eighteenth century, brickwork became more fashionable than rubble stone walling, but squared and finely tooled ashlar stonework remained the superior material.

Above Roman pigs (crude ingots) of Derbyshire lead have been found as far afield as Sussex. The material was highly prized for its unique qualities. As seen here at St Oswald's Church, Ashbourne, it can be used to cover roofs which have a very low pitch – an essential characteristic of Perpendicular Gothic architecture (1335–1530). Gerald Gregory, one of the county's most expert plumbers, is seen renewing the covering to the nave in milled lead, a material which is 90 per cent recycled.

Left Stone slate has also been used as a roof covering in the county since antiquity. This is a mitred valley at Unthank Hall Farm, Holmesfield. The slates' distinctive appearance identify them as being from one of the little quarries at Freebirch near Chesterfield. The wonderful ripple pattern is a result of water action – when sediment was laid down 300 million years ago on what was then a river bed. The roof was relaid by Sellors of Bakewell in 1994. The farmer is Mr John Lowe, whose family have been at Unthank Hall since 1676.

Left The great majority of stone roofs are made up of slates formed from riven sandstone and shaped to have rounded heads and square bottoms (see p. 24), but for small structures, massive rectangular slabs were sometimes used, which span from wall to wall and are fixed simply by virtue of weight and gravity. These ones are of gritstone and they roof the semi-detached privies in the gardens of the terraced houses that Sir Richard Arkwright built for his mill workers on Cromford Hill between 1776 and 1790.

Below The roof covering of part of the Manor House at Whitwell is a great rarity, the stone slates having been fashioned from the Magnesian Limestone on which the house sits and from which the walls are also made. Only one other such roof is known to survive, at nearby Barlborough Hall. This stone has a wonderful variety of colour in it – buff, pink and cream – and over the years acquires a most beautiful patina. Note the shaped copings to the raised gable parapets and the finial to the left-hand gable.

Top left   Georgian clay tiles at Melbourne. Their charming texture is a result of the irregularities caused by hand-moulding and uneven firing in the kiln.

Top right   Pantiles at Bolsover. The two courses of stone slates give stronger eaves with a better projection away from the wall than can be achieved with pantiles.

Lower left   Staffordshire blue tiles on a nailmaker's workshop in Belper. John Farey, in his *Study of Derbyshire* of 1811, writes: 'In the Pottery District of Staffordshire, a kind of plane Tiles for Buildings are manufactured, which have a very dark purple colour, very like new Cast Iron, being very sound and durable, are in great repute in southern parts of Derbyshire, to which they are brought by the Trent and Mersey and other canals.'

Lower right   An eighteenth-century house in Eckington with four courses of stone slates at the eaves. Even the ubiquitous Welsh slate when used like this gains a strong regional character.

Above Rubble walling, brought to courses, and sitting on a plinth of the living rock. A roadway in Whitwell has been made level by cutting into a Magnesian Limestone outcrop and then building up a retaining wall on top of it using the removed stone.

Left Architectural detailing and masons' tooling accentuate the beauty of this warm brown stone at Bakewell. The jamb (side) and lintel (top) of the doorway opening are brought forward from the face of the wall and given a fine tooled finish with what are called chisel-draughted margins – where the direction of the tooling is turned at right angles as a regular border strip. The walling is made up of fairly regular blocks, but not in exactly uniform course depths, comparatively roughly dressed to a pattern that is common in central Derbyshire. The face of each stone is divided into four and each quarter is given roughly parallel grooves, all facing into the midpoint of the stone.

Top left   Babington House, Wirksworth, where limestone and sandstone are used together. The grey walling stone is hard Carboniferous Limestone, quarried from the hillside on which it sits. The pink stone used for the quoins (corners) and windows is gritstone, which is softer and easier to work.

Top right   The head, sill, jambs and mullions of this window at Brassington are of Carboniferous Limestone but of a dolomitic variety, that is to say rich in magnesium carbonate. The stone was sought out for its ability to be shaped.

Lower left   A hidden delight is the steep hillside footpaths of the limestone gorge in Matlock Dale where Carboniferous Limestone blocks lock together to form massive retaining walls. Clusters of valerian spring from tight joints.

Lower right   The Royal Well at Matlock Bath is made from tufa. The sponge-like appearance of this material results from lime-rich spring water gradually building up a crust over the moss and grass of the ground over which it flows, until the vegetable matter becomes petrified.

Top left   Gritstone quoins (and waterchute) with Coal Measures sandstone walling at Eckington. This gritstone, although a fairly soft stone, is harder and more durable than the soft sandstone of the coalfield.

Top right   Soft as it may be, it can glow in the right light, as it does here at the Manor House, Dronfield.

Lower left   New Red Sandstone from Mayfield and over the county boundary in Hollington, Staffordshire, was used in and around Ashbourne. When first taken from the quarry it is very soft, but it becomes much harder on exposure to air. It was used to produce very fine ashlar, as here at the Grey House, Church Street (see p. 105).

Lower right   Although at first very much a secondary building material, brick has been used in Derbyshire since the fifteenth century. When changing fashion dictated brick as being superior to anything but ashlar, an economic arrangement was to use finely finished stonework for the architectural embellishment of brick buildings, as here at the Red House, Dronfield, of 1731.

Left The enthusiasm for brick, which had begun in London in Queen Anne's reign, and which reached Derbyshire by about 1730, led to the setting up of simple brick clamps (kilns) in fields near local clay pits. The idiosyncrasies of clays and brickmakers' methods led to a rich variety of colour and texture which gives Georgian brickwork much character and beauty. When built, this house in Wirksworth would have been symmetrical, five windows on the first and second floors and four on the ground floor. The imposition of a tax on windows led to the pattern seen today.

Below As the technology of brickmaking became less haphazard, the shape, texture and colour of bricks became much more regular and consistent. This led to them losing much of their beauty. The Victorians went in for decorative mouldings, which compensate for the loss of variety in surface texture. Glorious results of this enthusiasm can be seen in Ilkeston, as here at The Market Inn.

A further development of the use of clay came with glazed terracotta blocks. This architectural tour de force is at Swadlincote, a town which was built partly on the profits from salt-glazed clay and earthenware, and where pottery is still made.

Because terracotta blocks could be cast to much larger dimensions than brick, there was an economy in construction. However, one imagines that the complexities of the architectural decoration used here must have fully compensated for any saving in that direction.

Economy alone was clearly the driving force in the case of this wonderfully eccentric length of walling at Eckington, where crucible slag pot waste from the (once) nearby iron furnace was used to extend the height of a sandstone wall.

CHIMNEYS AND GUTTERS

One only has to look at modern houses without chimney-stacks to realize how much chimneys add to the look of a building. Less obvious is the contribution that gutters make, but close study reveals interesting local variations in traditions and styles. Roofscape is as prominent as landscape in the towns and villages of the Peak, where settlements are often seen from above.

The provision of chimneys when solid fuel is not the form of heating planned to be used is a problem. To have dummy chimney-stacks would be futile and dishonest, but who is to say that we will never again be dependent on solid fuel? Chimneys also play a valuable role in ventilating a house.

It may seem surprising but, as with chimneys, gutters have an important architectural as well as practical purpose, providing emphasis to the head of the wall, much as a cornice does. Traditionally, gutters are fixed by means of metal or timber brackets or stone corbelling straight against the stone or brick wall. The use of a timber board on to which gutter brackets are screwed is quite alien. Similarly, the junction between roof tiles or slates and the gable wall was never covered by boards.

Too often, new building takes no heed of local styles. A rash of painted or stained gutter boards or bargeboards produces a jarring note in the majority of the county's historic towns and villages.

This chapter reveals some regional variations which can be enjoyed and which can be taken into account when new buildings are being designed.

From mid-Derbyshire northwards the chimney-stacks of substantial houses are given a note of distinction by the use of stone chimney pots, some 3 ft tall or more. Made in two halves and carved out of solid stone, they are often held together with a copper cable.

The one in the foreground on p. 42 is on the Old Hall Hotel at Buxton. Beyond can be seen a range of brand new sandstone pots, shaped on a lathe, crowning the massive chimney-stacks of The Crescent.

The clays of south Derbyshire produced a range of products, including decorative chimney pots. Happily, the clays around Measham are still dug and fired to produce an amazing array of pot types, glorying in wildly improbable names such as Lancashire Bishop, Lady Broughton, Venetian Cap, Horned Can, Tee Can with Lid and Weemac. Although now in Leicestershire, Measham came within the county of Derbyshire until a boundary change in 1897.

In Old Glossop the native gritstone is shaped ingeniously to provide architectural interest to the roofs of that handsome old village. Note the staggered projecting stones up the side of the base of the chimney-stack. These thackstones provide a weathering junction with the roofing material.

External gutters are a relatively modern idea. In the Middle Ages the practice was to collect the water in lead-lined troughs behind parapets and shoot it out, well beyond the building, through spouts and gargoyles, or simply to have wide, overhanging eaves. This gritstone spout at Eckington is on a seventeenth-century building.

The earliest downpipes are in lead, often square in section, with boxes at the head to collect the water from the outlet. These boxes, called hopper heads, were, on the grandest buildings, given decorative castings and made into architectural features, but many more humble houses and cottages remained without downpipes until cast-iron goods became readily available.

Prior to the development of cast iron, timber troughs provided the means of collecting water externally at eaves level. This is still standard practice in the north of the county. The shaped lengths of Russian red deal are stacked, ready for purchase, at Albion Sawmills in Chesterfield. Around Chesterfield it is known as spouting. Further south, around Matlock, they are called launders. In the far north-west, around Glossop and New Mills, they are called trows. What is more surprising than the survival of the timber gutter is the extent of its use. Tens of thousands of cottages and terraced houses still have them and in those regions they are considered nothing out of the ordinary.

Different areas have their own traditions of fixing. At this house in Eckington the spouting is supported on paired timber brackets which are cantilevered out from the head of the stone wall. Generally the spouting and brackets are painted to match the window and door joinery colour scheme, but the inside of the trough is given several coats of bitumastic paint. In earlier days pitch or tar would have been used.

Spouting has the advantage of weighing less than cast iron but jointing is more problematical. A half-lap joint has to be used and made sound and waterproof with putty and bitumen.

Across the moors, in Glossop, the trows are generally supported on stone corbels. Plain or shaped, like these ones which have an ogee profile, they make a strong contribution to architectural composition.

Here, plain block corbels have been used intelligently by the designer of the new water treatment works at nearby Padfield to help integrate the building into its context.

Above   The development of the use of cast iron during
the early years of the nineteenth century allowed gutters
and rainwater pipes to be made of the same materials and
to have well-fitting joints and fixings, an opportunity
fully exploited by the Strutt family on their mills and
workers' houses at Belper. The brackets are designed to
allow for precise adjustment and they bear the
characteristic stamp of heavy engineering. The date of
their introduction is not known, but it has been
speculated that they may have been the brainchild of
William Strutt, the eldest son of patriarch Jedediah, who
inherited his father's mechanical ability and who was
among the first to design and build multi-storey fireproof
buildings.

Left   The simpler and more common wrought iron
bracket has its own charm. These are modern copies in
mild steel, which can be made up by any competent
blacksmith or metal worker. The curved support simply
rests against the stone or brickwork.

At the turn of the nineteenth century, some designers took full advantage of the decorative possibilities provided by the metal gutter bracket – as here in Bath Street, Ilkeston. The architect was Harry Tatham-Sudbury, who practised in Ilkeston between 1890 and 1942. While these wonderfully flamboyant brackets may owe something to the vernacular metal bracket, it must be admitted that they owe more to the influence of architects such as Voysey, Baillie-Scott and other taste formers of the Arts and Crafts movement.

Above Where there is no problem if walls get a little damp, such as in farm buildings, there is no need for gutters or down pipes, allowing, as at this barn, for a jolly pattern to be made from oversailing brickwork.

Left Here a rainwater pipe fixed on spacers casts a strong shadow, revealing an interesting walling tradition occurring in Derbyshire only in the far north-west. 'Watershot' walling required the face of each stone to incline outwards towards the top. There seems to be no practical reason behind this. The best explanation is that it was done purely for appearance, as often it only occurs on the public faces of a building.

Opposite Each area has its own details. This farm group at Ireton Wood has raised stone parapets at the gables, ending with projecting, shaped stones called kneelers. It is a precious patchwork of local tradition which we dilute at our cost.

DOORS
AND
WINDOWS

Nothing enhances the appearance of a house, chapel or factory more than its doors and windows, yet the legacy of Georgian and Victorian joinery in our towns and villages is being eroded at an alarming rate. Shiny white plastic and ginger-stained wood replacements are damaging the character of many of our old buildings. There is a need for a balancing view to the aggressive marketing of plastic and off-the-peg wooden replacements. For example, it is not understood that the quality of the Baltic pine from which most old joinery was made is incomparably better than anything that can be bought from the wood yard today, and old crown or cylinder glass has a liveliness and sparkle which makes modern float glass drab by comparison.

A lot of pleasure can be had from stopping and looking *at* doors and windows rather than just looking *through* them. We travel to stately homes to wonder at our architectural heritage, but to the enquiring eye there is much to enjoy closer to home. By acquiring a little knowledge about window and door styles it is possible to place a building in time and to discover something about the ways of life of former occupants.

Opposite An unaltered house at Eckington.

Top left   Doubtless this plain plank door in a simple stone doorway rarely gets a second look. It is the only one to survive in a long terrace of Georgian mill workers' houses in Glossop's High Street. Its survival is probably pure chance, yet how eloquently it speaks of its time.

Above   This plank door in Melbourne was made in 1994. It is a careful copy of the original and it is difficult to imagine any other type of door looking as good in the same opening. Care has been taken to use the correct wide planks and narrow scratch mouldings where they meet.

Left   Sir Richard Arkwright's builders took the plain plank door and added cross rails to the front face, presumably to give it a slightly up-market look. This door was made in 1991 for a house on Cromford Hill as a careful copy of a surviving door lower down the Hill.

Six-panel doors are recognized as the normal Georgian pattern, but they continued to be made by conservative-minded joiners right through the Victorian period. This pair in Ashbourne are of slightly different styles but, while different, their proportions and detailing are pleasing, a characteristic generally sadly lacking in their modern off-the-peg counterparts. The building they belong to, in Church Street, was originally a range of three houses constructed in about 1710. Early in the nineteenth century the range was converted to four houses and it was, doubtless, then that this pair of doors was inserted.

At the same time the, by then, old fashioned casement windows with arched heads were replaced by sashes. The brick arched heads to the old windows can still be seen either side of the doors. Note also the small proportion of the letterplate on the right-hand door. Victorian mail was of a quite different scale to our own. See p. 60 for a close-up of the lion head door knocker.

Top left A particularly robust kind of Georgian panelled door to one of the service buildings to Wirksworth Hall. This has no mouldings, but the panels are given emphasis by a strong, simple double chamfer to panels, rails (horizontal members) and stiles (vertical side members) alike. Its character is further emphasized by having no frame. It is hung on strong strap hinges on large pins built into the wall, and the door simply closes against a brick reveal. Arkwright's mill workers' houses (see p. 54) originally had no door frames either.

Above An alternative treatment was to have flush panels as at this house in New Mills. It has its own simple beauty. By the end of the eighteenth century the top two panels were sometimes glazed to give more light to the hallway.

Left Distinction is given to this doorway by the use of a semicircular fanlight with intersecting glazing bars.

By the mid-Victorian period, mouldings were becoming more pronounced. The depth and elaboration of moulded decorations was a status symbol, as was the use of decorative glass. This door is to a house in Spring Villas, Glossop. A similar range, Prospect Villas, dates from 1875. Before 1870, plain glass was given a pattern by acid etching. After 1870, the cheaper method of producing a frosted appearance by sandblasting had been developed.

The finely dressed Tuscan pilasters to the doorway, the arched head with its keystone, the pyramidal-topped stone gateposts and the decorative garden gate combine to give a splendid sense of entry to what is quite a modest dwelling.

Georgian and Victorian doors were invariably painted, unless they were made of an expensive hardwood, which was rare. However, Victorian doors were sometimes 'grained' to imitate hardwoods, a fashion that persisted up to the First World War.

This Victorian door in Eckington is given great distinction by the splendid trellised porch. The pierced gable gives a hint of Gothic taste, as do the little projections at the top of the trellis (see p. 61 for a detail). Porches such as this are now becoming very rare and the few that remain deserve to be lovingly cared for.

No joinery, no matter how fine the quality of the wood, can survive without being painted regularly. One of the imagined advantages of off-the-peg doors, which are sold in DIY shops and which are made of exotic hardwood with a stained finish, is that they require little or no maintenance other than a further coat of stain once in a while. However, now that these doors have been in place for a few years, it is rapidly becoming apparent that they soon lose their original lustre and, once dirty and faded, further applications of stain do little to improve their appearance.

The Victorians took Georgian details like wedge lintels and made them uniquely their own. The age is characterized by technical innovation and a delight in decoration. The lintels to this house in George Street, Riddings, are, most unusually, of cast iron, made in the Oakes family foundry which was established just outside the village in 1802. The central panel, which represents a keystone, is decorated with an oak-apple motif. The very simple four-panel door is the only one to survive in the street. The arched lintel over the entrance to the passageway (tunnel entrance) to the rear is also cast iron, as is, amazingly, the structure of the bay window (see p. 78).

A

B

C

D

E

F

G

H

Numberplates, knockers, letterplates, knobs and handles all add interest, variety and character to a door. Some towns or parts of towns have their own distinctive style of numberplate dating from when houses were first given numbers. In some places this was not until surprisingly late, for example after 1890, but we know that the cast-iron numberplates at Long Row, Belper, pre-date the coming of the railway in 1839 because where the line cuts across the street, in a deep cutting, it necessitated the demolition of some houses (see p. 134), and those numbers are missing.

A Applied numerals on a plank door in Glossop, overpainted.

B A painted numeral on a wooden plaque in Melbourne.

C A cast-iron numeral plaque in Belper.

D Another Belper cast-iron plaque, at 17 Long Row.

E A Victorian bat door knocker and letterplate.

F A modern cast aluminium numeral plaque, made in a small foundry in Nottinghamshire.

G A lion door knocker and numeral plaque at Church Street, Ashbourne.

H A wooden door knob and cast-iron knocker at Melbourne.

A cast-iron numeral plaque at Eckington.

Windows can often reveal the age of a building and sometimes the use to which rooms were put. This seventeenth-century window facing on to the churchyard at Bakewell proclaims, without any ambiguity, the use to which the room behind was once put, as the words 'CHEESE ROOM' painted on its lintel declare. Cheese rooms, having a single window, were exempt from window tax (see p. 65).

Opposite   In central Derbyshire the staircases of eighteenth-century houses were often lit by astonishingly tall tiers of leaded lights. Because they invariably occur to the rear of buildings they are rarely open to view. This one in Wirksworth can be seen because the back of the building faces on to Church Walk.

Windows can also say something about the social status or aspirations of the original residents. These windows to a range of Georgian houses in Wirksworth could, however, confuse. They are a version of a fashionable Palladian style, called a Venetian window, but a very simplified version. The most likely reason why they were built like this, on otherwise humble houses, was because they housed servants of the hall and lined the route that the master and mistress would take to church.

Nevertheless, the masons who constructed the window openings were conscious of the importance of proportion. The distance between the top of the arched opening and the sill is exactly equivalent to the distance between the outer jambs of the side windows; in other words the windows fit exactly into a square. Until earlier this century the windows were glazed with leaded lights.

Above The far left-hand windows on the first and second floors of this Georgian house in Wirksworth's market-place are fakes. They were either built like that and given painted-on sashes to give symmetry and balance to the façade or, more likely, they were bricked up at a later date. Either way the payment of window tax was minimized. This form of gathering revenue was first introduced in 1696. The amounts of duty payable and the categories of buildings on which it was levied were increased at various times, including 1710, 1766, 1798 and 1800 (see p. 39).

Left Another Georgian blind window. It is a measure of the visual sensitivity of the age that so much trouble was taken, with even the depth of the imitation overlapping sashes being built in. It can be seen that no such niceties bothered those who, at a later date, bricked up the doorway partly shown to the right.

A rare and precious survival, in Ashbourne, of a Georgian sash window, complete with its original glass and panelled shutters. The sash window was a revolutionary development in building construction. It is said to have come to England from Holland in about 1670. The first time sash windows are known to have been used in any number was at Chatsworth, in 1676. Gradually the sash replaced the casement window, and it remained the most popular form of fenestration for more than two centuries.

Note the delightful little pierced openings in the top panels of the shutters, which provide a glimmer of light in the room when the shutters are closed. Notice also the brilliance of the glass, catching the light and reflections of the street scene.

The sash window was made possible through an improvement in glass manufacture, which allowed larger panes to be cut from blown discs or cylinders. Spun crown glass or cylinder glass gives a window a wonderful sparkle and liveliness, as can be seen in these 'Yorkshire' sash windows in Melbourne (above) and Whitwell (left). The Yorkshire sash is a regional variation, with the sliding part moving horizontally on a runner, rather than vertically on weighted cords. It is more common in North Derbyshire and was never used for houses with architectural pretensions.

The process of replacing old-fashioned casement windows, which had small panes of diamond-shaped or rectangular glass held together with lead cames, with larger-paned sash windows, continued into this century, as photographs taken in the early 1900s reveal (see p. 71).

A development of the cylinder method of glass production, in 1838, allowed larger panes to be used. The early Victorian margin light pattern of sash windows, seen here at Eckington, is an attractive variation, made possible by the new pane dimensions. Sometimes the small square corner panes are of coloured glass.

The glazing bars of later sash windows are very slim and fine. The thickness of glazing bars, or astragals as they are sometimes called, gives an indication of the age of a window. Those used in the earliest sashes of the late seventeenth and early eighteenth centuries are broad and chunky. They became progressively thinner through the eighteenth century until by the 1800s they could be as slim as three quarters of an inch.

Another clue to age is whether the sashes have 'horns' – the short projections of the stiles on each side of the top sash. Generally, eighteenth-century windows lack them. Meeting rails – the horizontal members at the bottom of the top sash and the top of the bottom sash – are slimmer when there are no horns.

The sash remains a perfectly sensible and practical window, provided that it is painted intelligently and its cords occasionally overhauled. This house, built in 1991 at Calver, is by no means a slavish copy of an old style, but its sash windows help to integrate it into the historical village scene.

The window surrounds are of reclaimed golden brown coarse gritstone from near Glossop, cut and dressed by the banker masons whose business is described on p. 22. They are set in rubble Carboniferous Limestone, roughly brought to courses. The deeper windows in the recessed section are set in the same limestone, but here it is regularly coursed with a fine ashlar sawn finish. The house was built as a speculative venture by Andrew Whitham, a small-scale developer and builder who works in partnership with architect Russell Light.

The timber casement also remains a sensible and practical window, provided that it is properly maintained. Double-glazing can be achieved quite easily (and economically) by secondary glazing within the depth of the window reveal.

 This house in the model colliery village of New Bolsover retains its original joinery. It is one of 200 houses built by the Bolsover Colliery Company in 1891, using its own bricks. An 'endless' rope transported tubs from the clay hole near the pithead stocks to the brickworks. The company determined to offer its workforce high-standard housing, in contrast with most miners' cramped and unhealthy homes. It was the first model village to be built by a mining company. Three types of houses were constructed. The three-storey house, with an attic dormer window, was originally rented at 3s 6d. The two-storey type was 3s and semi-detached villas were provided for the colliery officials. The architect was Arthur Brewill of Nottingham. The charm of model villages lies largely with the consistency of architectural detail, especially in the doors and windows.

Above This casement window is interesting in two respects. It has no central timber mullion, the two casements simply joining in a half lap against each other, and it retains its external shutter, which closes neatly into the deep brick reveal. External and internal shutters provide excellent thermal and sound insulation, as well as security.

A photograph taken in about 1906 shows that some, if not all, of the mullioned windows on the millworkers' houses on Cromford Hill retained, at that date, their original leaded lights. On one side the small rectangular panes were leaded directly into grooves in the stonework and on the other side of the stone mullion the leaded lights were fitted within a small vertically sliding sash window. One original window of this type survives on the first floor of No. 3 North Street. The windows also retained their original boarded shutters, the fixings for which can be seen in the stone window jambs.

Left The neat timber casements, which now occur in a number of houses on the Hill, were presumably installed by the Arkwright Estate (which retained ownership of most of the village until the 1920s) to replace the original leaded lights.

Above In the first half of the nineteenth century the iron-making companies, such as Handyside in Derby and Butterley in Ripley, used native ore to manufacture an astonishingly wide range of cast-iron goods, including window frames. This tiny casement is at Short Row, Belper. Note its external pin-and-socket hinges and wrought-iron stay.

Left A thirty-five pane cast-iron window in a cottage at Ireton Wood near Kirk Ireton. The opening part is a minute, two-pane, casement in the centre.
   Cast-iron windows were generally placed near to the front face of the wall and often without sills. The opening size and arched head is determined by the size of the window bought 'off the shelf'. See how the original cylinder glass gives the window brilliance and emphasizes its particular character.

Mass-produced iron windows continued to be used in the county's industrial buildings through the whole of the nineteenth century, including the monumental tenement lace factories at Long Eaton. This is Whiteley's factory of 1883. The last one to be built was Bridge Mills (see p. 133), in 1902. Some windows were made in the town's own iron foundry. They flood the buildings with light and provide the rhythm which gives these utilitarian buildings much of their stark beauty.

Long Eaton developed as a lace-making centre late on in the nineteenth century, as a satellite to nearby Nottingham, linked by canal, road and railway. Land was relatively cheap and plentiful, thereby providing the space needed for these heroically large-scale buildings. Good brick clay was available close by. A field near the canal was known as Brick Kiln Close in 1832.

Many of the town's best buildings were designed by the local architect John Sheldon. Keith Reedman's excellent book on the town describes how Sheldon came from a family who had a joinery business in the early nineteenth century. In 1860 he became a builder and made his own bricks. By 1880 he was part-time surveyor and architect to the Long Eaton Local Board and, later, to the Urban District Council. His two sons, John and James, joined the practice, which continued until the latter's death in 1930.

Harrington Mills, seen above, is one of their finest buildings. The rhythm of the multi-storeyed windowed bays, between simple projecting giant pilasters, is given counterpoint by the rhythm of the projecting turnpike stair towers, their strong, largely unbroken, brick walls punctured only by relatively small windows and taking-in doors.

Left   Lace 'beams', which carry the warp thread in the manufacture of lace, spied through a window of one of the single-storey factories.

The mills and factories of Derbyshire are a major contribution to its architectural heritage and it is good that one of the best buildings of recent years is a cutlery factory, at Hathersage. The architect, Michael Hopkins, has taken local building materials and used them without any falsity to make an elegant workshop that speaks of today. The windows appear simply as voids — reinforcing the visual solidity of the walls (see also p. 6). The design is a powerful demonstration that there is no need to imitate historical styles for a building to fit into the local scene.

To achieve a design of this high order there is a need not just for a talented architect but also for a patron of creativity and vision — in this case it was the master cutler and designer David Mellor. It is particularly good that the building lies within the Peak District National Park, where the demands of conservation are often misinterpreted as being a 'dead-hand'.

The eminent architectural historian Sir Nikolaus Pevsner once observed that 'the English cannot live without bay windows'. These are at Buxton (opposite) and Ilkeston (above). The Victorians took the form and made it their own, glorying in decoration and ingenuity. The bays at Buxton belong to a range in Bath Road that was built in two phases around 1878. Note the crenellations (miniature battlements) around the head of the first-floor bay and to the top of the doorway. At St Mary's Street, Ilkeston, the arched heads to the ground-floor windows have been given little decorative rosettes. Note also the elaborate moulded brick frieze between the bay windows and the eaves of the roof.

Above   Although difficult to detect under its painted finish, this bay window at Swadlincote is constructed from cast and fired clay-ware, presumably made locally. The production of such fruity Corinthian capitals must have been a considerable technical challenge.

Left   At George Street, Riddings, it is not just door lintels which were cast in the nearby Oake's Iron Works (see p. 59) but also the structural units of the bay windows. As Frank Nixon observed in his *Industrial Archaeology of Derbyshire*: 'Until the advent of cheap steel, cast iron was put to uses which present-day iron founders find difficult to credit. The "Era of Cast Iron" was inaugurated very largely by such firms as Ebenezer-Smith of Chesterfield, Butterley, Andrew Handyside of Derby, Staveley, Stanton and James Oakes at Riddings.'

The sheer exuberance and ingenuity of the Victorian designer-builder is wonderfully illustrated in Bath Street, Ilkeston, where, if one lifts one's head above the banal modern shop fronts, one can see how the window can be exploited to its full decorative potential.

SIGNS, NAMEPLATES AND GRAVESTONES

The basic purpose of signs, nameplates and gravestones is to provide information, but the best ones also give visual delight and sometimes even the odd chuckle.

To the inquisitive eye they can reveal much more than they might, at face value, seem to. A street name, for instance, may give a clue to why a route exists. For example: Brikkin Lane (the way to the site of a brick kiln), Steeple Grange (the steep hill which leads up to the site of a monastic grange, or farm) and Summer Lane (a route only comfortably passable in the dry summer months).

One needs to learn to 'read' the urban landscape rather as one needs to learn to read a language. It can well repay the trouble.

Opposite   Scarthin Bookshop at Cromford (see pp. 86 and 87), seen across the mill pond which lies behind the market-place. This part of Cromford was once a separate settlement. 'Scarthin' means nicks or cuts; that is, passes through or over the rock.

Pub signs can be a mine of information and often romance. The Royal Oak at Mayfield is a Restoration building. The name alludes to Charles II's hiding place in the Boscobel Oak 30 miles or so to the south-west in nearby Shropshire. The simple timber post from which the sign hangs was once a common sight on Derbyshire pubs, but few survive because the horizontal timber was built into stone or brickwork, with its strength deriving from the cantilever effect. Renewal of the timber is difficult because it has to be sunk well into the thickness of the wall. For this reason, raking brackets were sometimes added.

The pleasure to be gained from being able to recognize the significance or origin of a name is considerably increased through the feeling one can experience in spotting that someone else has got it wrong. The brewery appears to believe The Blue Stoops at Dronfield is derived from the name for a drinking vessel. However, Derbyshire folk are perfectly familiar with the word stoop, which is still in use, to describe a post or bollard. The Dronfield manorial court records for 1757 to 1857 reveal that the manor court was held, at times, at The Blue Posts. In the days when brewing was but one of the commercial activities of a farm or workshop, the fact that beer could be bought was advertised by some kind of symbol, such as painting the posts of the doorway, or freestanding posts outside, a bright colour.

The splendid bracket for the hanging sign at The George, Belper, speaks of a long tradition of fine ironwork in Derbyshire. The county benefited from the genius of England's most talented eighteenth-century blacksmith, Robert Bakewell. After apprenticeship in London he practised his art in Derbyshire between 1718 and his death in 1752. His most famous work is the 'birdcage' or arbour of 1706–11 in the gardens of Melbourne Hall. His apprentice, Benjamin Yates, took over the management of his business in 1749–50 and in 1776 William Yates took over from Benjamin. This sign bracket is in their family tradition. The bracket for the hanging sign of the former Bull's Head in Queen Street, Derby, which is attributed to Bakewell's workshop, can be seen in Derby Museum.

The White Swan at Melbourne has two signs of some distinction. The painted wall sign has a moulded plaster frame, which wraps around the corner of the building. A photograph taken in the 1880s shows that, at that time, the frame contained a lettered sign, simply 'The White Swan Inn', but it must surely have been made for a pictorial sign such as the one which now adorns the building. The hanging sign is a twentieth-century addition, but it is no less attractive for that. It is good that each age can add its own stamp on to the local scene. Each building is made up of layers of history. The lintel over the doorway tells us that the inn was built in 1682 for someone with the initials W.E. Such clues are an invitation to research and discovery.

The sign for Scarthin Bookshop, Cromford, reflects the wit and individuality of its owner, bookseller and publisher David Mitchell. Husband and wife blacksmith-designer team Simon and Julia Vaughan developed a theme devised by local joiner and customer Jacob Butler. The head is that of Amalthea, horn-bearer and nursemaid of Zeus. The objects falling from her horn, in addition to books, are some of the belongings frequently misplaced by the owner, including spectacles and dentures. The Japanese lettering spells out 'bookshop' and the two latin tags loosely translate as 'book in hand, freedom in mind' and 'what you seek you bring'.

Above The lettering for the bookshop fascia is made of applied characters cut by fretsaw, from a letter type devised by the late David Offley, a cabinetmaker who lived at Shipley Common near Ilkeston. The business was established in 1974 and has become renowned far beyond Derbyshire as an outstanding source of new and secondhand books.

Scarthin was once a little settlement, separate from Cromford, which became absorbed into the village when Arkwright developed a market-place west of the River Derwent.

Left On the south side of the market-place, Tony Carline runs a butcher's shop. As the hanging sign proudly proclaims, it is a family business. Tony took over the management of it 17 years ago from his father, Anthony Carline, who moved his butchery business here from Matlock Bath more than 50 years ago. Although the slaughterhouse behind the shop had to be closed in the 1960s, the meat sold is still from locally reared stock.

This band of decorative red and white brickwork incorporates, generously spaced out, the name of the institution which the building originally housed when it was erected in Ilkeston in 1884 by the (Anglican) Young Men's Mutual Improvement Society. The institute was designed by J.H. Kilford, one of the board of governors. It stands just off the market-place.

Each letter is a separate moulded terracotta plaque, two courses of brickwork deep. The characters are raised against a ground of moulded florets, which catch the light and shade.

The population of Ilkeston more than doubled between 1871 and 1891. Its growth resulted from a change from agriculture to manufacturing and coal-mining. Although coal had been won from surface deposits since at least the fourteenth century, it was not until the construction of the Erewash and Nutbrook canals that it could be exported economically. Several brickyards were established in association with the coalfield. By the end of the nineteenth century the town had been virtually rebuilt, all in local brick (see also p. 39).

The 1841 census records twenty-two brickmakers in Ilkeston ranging in age from 13 to 86.

Swadlincote was another community where coal extraction had occurred in the Middle Ages in a small way, but emerged as a major industry in the nineteenth century. The new industrial society was supported by mutual co-operation and interdependence typified by the prominence of the town's handsome Co-operative Store.

These glazed terracotta signs, incorporated into the parapets of branch number nine of the Burton on Trent Co-operative Society Ltd in West Street, Swadlincote, are a manifestation of the significance of that movement.

Another Co-operative Stores sign, here at the model colliery village of New Bolsover which lies below Bolsover Castle (see pp. 70 & 136) is carved in sandstone but set in colliery bricks. The Co-operative stores at New Bolsover was branch number twelve of the Pleasley and Pleasley Hill Co-operative Society Ltd. Arthur Brewill, FRIBA, of Nottingham was the architect and it was built between 1891 and 1894 as part of a complex of houses and community facilities provided for 200 families by the Bolsover Colliery Company. In addition to the stores there was an institute, a school and community centre, public baths, an orphanage and allotments.

Model villages had been developed for workers in other industries earlier, such as at Saltaire near Bradford, for those employed in the woollen trade, and at Port Sunlight in Cheshire, built around 1888 for the soap firm Lever, but New Bolsover was the first model colliery village. It is now a conservation area and survives relatively intact, the only major loss being the village school and community centre which lined one side of the large green around which the housing is laid out. The colliery closed in 1993.

A major scheme of repair and enhancement was carried out 'at the model village by Bolsover District Council between 1993 and 1995, and there are plans to create a museum of coal-mining community life.

Above The vigour, ambition and pride of industrial and mercantile life in the Victorian era is manifest in the decorative signs which still adorn their buildings, even when the purposes for which those buildings were constructed have long gone. This splendid sign for the New Mills branch of the Manchester and County Bank, in the tympanum of its doorway, is as sharp as the day when it was carved in 1862. Sadly, the building as a whole has not fared so well.

Left Pride in ownership reached down to the artisan, who may have been the first generation to revel in the status of owner-occupier. This gatepost in Bath Street, Buxton, has the house name carved around the top of an incised trefoil.

This sign in Bolsover shows how the tradition did not die entirely in the twentieth century. The charming bas-relief of a Bakelite telephone was produced in about 1950 when a small automatic telephone exchange was built in the High Street. Prior to that the exchange for the town had operated from the sitting room of Mrs Anne Hall's house at No. 41 Hilltop. The telephone equipment sat on the little packing case, in which it had been delivered, in the centre of the floor.

For an exchange to be opened there had to be a minimum of ten subscribers. The role of a small town telephonist in those days was such that Mrs Hall and her assistants, daughters Gertrude and Caroline, could carry on with their normal household duties unless called by the bell. People who were not subscribers could come to the house and make a call from the sitting room. The only time when the new facility was heavily used was when there was a disaster at the nearby Markham Colliery.

The sign is already a period piece. Such minor expressions of pride in local facilities add a dimension of quality and care in appearances which can bring a smile to the weary passer-by.

Cast iron lends itself well to signs and nameplates. This small and curious plate above the doorway of a house in Bridge Street, Belper, once identified the home of a member of the Strutt Mills fire brigade. Presumably the plate was to assist in a call-out. A photograph of the brigade survives, showing eleven firemen, replete in brass helmets, in the yard of the West Mill. Presumably ten other plates were once to be found on the houses of the other members of the brigade. The 'engine' appears to be a box on wheels, containing the hoses. A large hand-pump was stabled nearby.

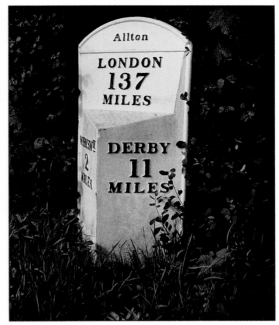

James Haywood's Phoenix Foundry and John Harrison's Foundry, both of Derby, produced a large number of cast-iron mileposts in the nineteenth century, many of which can still be seen along the roads of the county and within town centres.

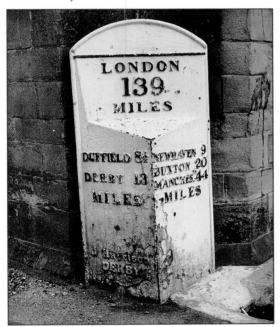

This one stands against the town hall at Wirksworth and this, on the right, against the town hall at Ashbourne.

The information on them provides an insight into earlier patterns of travel. For example, the distance to Newhaven is given equal prominence to the distances to Derby and Manchester. Today it has little or no significance as a destination or resting place, its large posting inn in an otherwise agricultural hamlet no longer fulfilling the role of being the final place for refreshment before setting off across the wilds of the White Peak.

Above   Street name signs can often tell something about the places and the times in which they were made. The incised Roman lettering on a terrace of sandstone buildings in New Mills is in the Georgian tradition and gives a clue to its early nineteenth-century origin, although at a quick glance the range looks thoroughly Victorian, or even Edwardian, because of later inserted shop fronts.

Left   At the other end of the same street is a cast-iron nameplate, probably cast in one of the town's own foundries towards the end of the nineteenth century or even later. The original role of the street is self-explanatory.

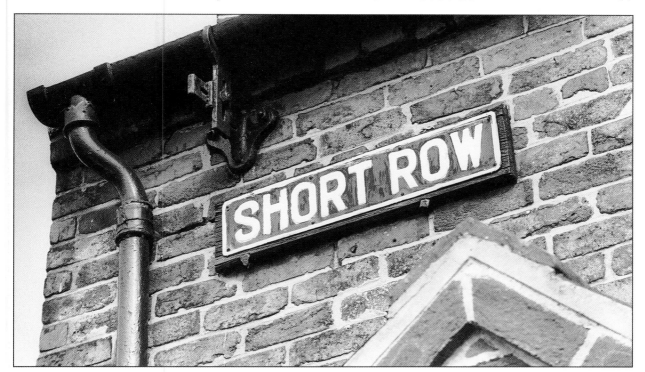

This metal nameplate on a timber backing is on the smallest range of Strutt's industrial housing at Belper. It is fixed with square, hand-cut nails made in one of the town's nailmakers' workshops, which were numerous in the eighteenth century when there was a substantial export trade of nails to the American colonies.

Some town centre streets in Wirksworth have enamelled street nameplates, with white lettering on a dark blue background. Blind Lane gets its name simply from the fact that it is a cul-de-sac, ending at the entrance to Church Walk.

A cast nameplate in Ashbourne. Frith's Yard leads off the town's principal street through a tunnel entrance. It is one of a number of such alleys which were created to give access to yards developed behind the built-up frontages, within the medieval long and narrow property divisions called burgage plots.

Buxton has some robust and distinctive cast-iron nameplates. Although now partly obscured by the darkening of the surface of the stone, the name of the terrace can still just be made out in the carved lettering along a band course below the nameplate.

A carved and painted sign in Melbourne elegantly turns the corner of South Street within a stone band course between brickwork made up entirely of 'headers' – the ends of bricks. These will be what are called snapped headers, that is to say bricks which have been cut to a short length to enable a tight curve to be built. The name of the next road, Alma Street, gives the clue to the date of the development of this part of the town. The battle of Alma was in 1854. It was a turning point in the Crimean War, which ended two years later.

Gravestones can tell a rich story and often very beautifully. Melbourne benefited from being only 10 miles from Charnwood Forest in Leicestershire where the quarries of Swithland produced slate of a quality that allowed the very finest of lettering to be carried out. This elegantly cut stone stands in the graveyard of Melbourne's Baptist Church. Being of nonconformist persuasion did not prevent Thomas Earp of King's Newton from having a positively florid memorial when he died at the age of eighty in 1822. The letter carver, Pratt, was understandably proud enough to record his own name.

The verse at the base of the stone speaks of the quality of life to be expected in Georgian times for those who exceeded their biblical span:

> Tis but a few whose years amount
> To the three score years and ten
> And all beyond that short account
> Is labour toil and pain

On the margins of gritstone country, at Bakewell, the untimely demise of Thomas Stratton in 1842 is recorded in a very handsome, architecturally distinguished headstone. The inscription tells of his accidental death, 'suddenly cut off in the Prime of Life and Vigour of Health', while working on the north arch of the church tower. The profile of the top of the stone echoes the crenellations at the top of the tower – no doubt a deliberate tribute chosen by his fellow masons, whose part in the memorial is recorded at the base:

Erected by a few of his
Fellow Workmen.

In the overgrown part of the churchyard of Eckington's twelfth-century parish church stands this splendid headstone. It is now a monument more to the taste of the high Victorian period than to the person whose mortal remains lie below it, since the inscription in the central panel of white imported marble is almost obliterated by erosion.

A rare grave marker made in cast iron is preserved at the nearby Renishaw Ironworks. It was cast for Thomas Appleby, a local man who bought the ironworks in 1782. The people of Eckington and Renishaw worked local deposits of high-grade iron ore since at least the seventeenth century and probably before.

What a joy it is to come across a modern gravestone of local material and by a lettercutter as expert as Pratt of Melbourne. This is one of a number of good modern memorials to be found in the churchyard of All Saints Church, Turnditch – a circumstance which results from the discernment of the vicar of the time as much as the families of those commemorated. The artist is sculptor and lettercutter John Shaw of Market Rasen, Lincolnshire. The gritstone is from Stancliffe Quarry, Darley Dale. Photograph by John Shaw.

Roads, Pavements and Paths

Ancient paving is rare because before the Georgian period most roads, squares and paths were simply dirt or, more often, mud. Where it does survive it is very precious, yet surprisingly there is no system to give it legal protection as there is for historic buildings, not even in conservation areas. What little does exist is under threat as never before, with cable television contractors joining the ranks of the gas, water, electricity and telephone road gangs. Also, where paving is replaced or newly laid following the exclusion of vehicles, 'anywhere' types of material are often used, thereby further diminishing the distinctive character of towns and villages. The old causeys (pavements) of Derbyshire are under threat.

As with roofing and walling, each area had its own tradition of paving, based on locally available materials. Clay paving bricks are to be found in the south of the county; limestone and gritstone setts in the centre and north-west; and sandstone setts and paving slabs in the north-east. What survives is a little regarded but important part of the county's heritage. Study of it can give interest and enjoyment by enabling us to find clues to past ways of life.

Even rarer than historic paving is documentary evidence for its age. For the area of cobbles outside Ashbourne's Elizabethan Grammar School, later extended along the front of the Grey House, documents survive to tell us that they were first laid in 1607 and were taken from the River Dove at Hanging Bridge. They were extensively repaired between 1727 and 1732 when more cobbles were taken from the river bed. The records note that payment was made for ale 'for the men to go into the water to pick stones for paving'.

Evidence for the earliest use of cobble paving in the county was discovered in 1979 in an archaeological dig of a Roman Site at Carsington, where riverine pebble paving to the floors of rooms was found.

Top left   Sandstone setts outside Ashbourne Town Hall.

Top right   Paving can explain the use of a yard or ginnel. This glazed brick channel is in Shakespeare's Yard in the centre of Ashbourne. Shakespeare was a Victorian butcher. At the top of the yard a slaughterhouse remained in use until 1978. It doesn't take much imagination to work out what the channel was for. It was a never to be forgotten experience to come face to face with a beast in the tight confines of the yard's tunnel entrance.

Lower left   This tunnel entrance leads to Railway Yard in Ashbourne. It is paved in blue clay paving bricks with indentations that make it look rather like a massive chocolate bar.

Lower right   Carboniferous Limestone makes hard-wearing paving which over the years acquires a polished finish. The earliest use of it is in the form seen here at a causey in Cromford. Irregular blocks are fitted together like mini crazy-paving. This is called pitching.

Top left   Here, limestone pitchings have been used to form a drainage channel around the perimeter of a former malthouse in Crown Yard, Wirksworth.

Top right   A later form of limestone paving is regularly sized setts and kerbs. These are in The Dale, Wirksworth, just a stone's throw from Dale Quarry where sett makers worked until the 1930s.

Lower left   Most limestone setts are 4-inch cubes, but these in Chapel Lane are 10 × 5 inches. They positively glow in bright sunlight.

Lower right   Gritstone is less hard wearing but easier to work and was made into larger setts. The road which serves the eighteenth-century mill workers' terraced houses at Long Row Belper is entirely surfaced with them. The gritstone bollards protected garden railings from cartwheels.

Top left   Happily, Glumangate in Chesterfield retains its large sandstone setts. Study of them reveals a beautiful range of colours. The stone almost certainly comes from the outcrop on which Chesterfield sits.

Top right   In Bolsover the local Magnesian Limestone is used for generously broad kerbs with tarmac pavements. Tarmac is not a pretty material, but it is often a good, low-key paving for small towns and villages where, historically, market squares and causeys were made simply of compacted dirt or stone hoggin and where any sort of fancy paving looks out of place.

Lower left   When new paving needs to be laid there is generally no problem about following local traditions if the will is there. These gritstone setts and Yorkstone flags were laid by New Mills Town Council in 1989 to provide access to its newly formed heritage centre, off a formerly unmade trackway.

Lower right   Red and blue paving bricks in Melbourne.

It may be stretching the scope of this chapter to its limits, but if one stands in this entry in Melbourne and looks up, another form of paving (or rather flooring) can be seen – the underside of a lime-ash floor.

Rather as a modern concrete floor slab is made, a slurry was poured on to shuttering and left to set. In Melbourne the slurry was made of burnt gypsum (plaster of Paris), ash from a lime kiln and other aggregates, like crushed brick. The shuttering can be reed, as here, or riven laths, laid on rafters. Different areas had their own recipes. Around Brassington, waste spar from lead mining was used; around Matlock, ash from lead furnaces was mixed with blood, according to John Farey, writing in 1811.

Lime-ash floors were used extensively in the Midlands in the seventeenth and eighteenth centuries, many of which survive.

The shop front can be a major visual 'event' in the street scene, but to appreciate this it is sometimes necessary to step back and take in the whole view. This grand set piece in Spring Gardens, Buxton, is a good case in point. From a casual walk down the street one might look at nothing more than a piece of china in the window, but cross the road and look at it four square on and the whole ensemble is revealed as a grand, high Victorian, commercial composition, perfectly intact down to the rainwater pipe.

The development of this part of Spring Gardens was carried out in about 1880 and the shop front is probably the original. The lettering on the fascia is made up of individual pottery characters with a gilt finish, which date from 1903, when the present china and glass business succeeded an earlier china and glass store.

High Street chemists tend to have particularly good shop fronts and often long pedigrees. Payne's, at Wirksworth, is distinguished by its original double bow windows, as well as its amusing name. The shop front probably dates from when a pharmacy was first established here in 1756. The current business was set up by Ben Payne in 1935. He was succeeded by his son, John, who in turn has handed over to his son Nicholas, who qualified as a pharmacist in 1988.

The first thing that catches the eye at Finlay McKinlays' pharmacy in Glossop is the ducal warrant sign. The centre of new Glossop was known as Howard Town, when it was first developed by the 12th Duke of Norfolk, Lord of the Manor of Glossop, in 1838.

The present business is run by Noel Oliver and his wife Edith, whose father, Finlay McKinlay, gave it his name in 1912. They are seen here with their daughters Pamela and Fay (the latter a Cambridge graduate in chemistry), and grandchildren Alec and Kay. It has been a pharmacy since at least the 1860s.

The architects for the duke's development were Weightman and Hadfield of Sheffield. The large architectural practice of Hadfield, Cawkwell and Davidson, which operates from Sheffield today, is the same firm. It claims to be the oldest continuously practising architectural firm in the country.

A

B

C

D

E

F

G

H

A David and Beverley Warhurst outside their sweet shop in Glossop, the window displays of which must mesmerize every child who passes.

B Margery Thompson at the door of her ladies' boutique, The Spotted Penguin, in Glossop.

C A customer leaving Moran's opticians in New Mills holding her new spectacles.

D Alan Wilkes by his handsomely painted delicatessen in New Mills.

E Nadya Kemp holding a tray of her delicious bread made in the little bakery at the back of her shop in Eckington.

F Roger French standing by a selection of the goods stocked in his traditional ironmonger's at Eckington. Screws are kept in tins made by Mr Johnson the ironmonger and tinsmith who ran the shop up until the 1930s.

G A cyclist passing Sid Gregson's Welcome Câfé in Melbourne.

H Stewart Clowes by the doorway to his pharmacy in Buxton. In the upper part of the window stand giant decorative carboys holding coloured liquid, once a standard element in chemists window displays.

What a great deal of variety and human interest is given to the street scene of our small towns by the family run shop.

Shops
and
Shop Fronts

The pleasure that the small shopkeeper gains from independence and the provision of individual service shines out from these photographs. The shops are outposts of individuality and character in both the human and the architectural sense.

The small scale of the shop front is in proportion to the town or village centre — a fact that is emphasized when larger shop fronts of corporate businesses are introduced.

Yet the small village and town centre shopkeeper is an endangered species. The demand for convenience shopping with easy parking is, inevitably, putting at risk large numbers of traditional shops, even though their demise is widely regretted.

These photographs celebrate shops that have survived. They show what a wealth of visual interest traditional shop fronts give to the High Street. They also provide a glimpse of the human interest that lies behind them. Napoleon is supposed to have said 'The English are a nation of shopkeepers.' Good, let's keep it that way.

Anyone who passes down Matlock Street in Bakewell in the winter months and does not spot the display outside Skidmore's vegetable and game shop must be extremely unobservant. It is a remarkable sight, although one which was much less remarkable in years gone by.

Michael Skidmore, together with brothers Graham and John, run the business that was begun by their father John when he was invalided out of the Army at the end of the First World War. The game comes from a number of local estates, including the Duke of Rutland's at nearby Haddon Hall. It can include pheasant, grouse, partridge, duck, goose, woodcock, teal, pigeon, hare and rabbit.

John's son, Nigel, who works at the supermarket over the road, can pluck a duck in less than 3 minutes and fifty brace (100) of pheasants in 2 hours.

Above   To be able to get really good bread straight from the oven is a joy unknown to many city dwellers. The customers of Graeme Pomfret at Fred Platt & Sons, Glossop, can even see it being made. Graeme started to work for Platts 17 years ago, at first as a Saturday boy. Within 7 years he had bought the business, retaining the name as well as the original fittings and equipment. Work starts at 5.30 a.m. and by 10.00 a.m. he is delivering his delicious bread in a laden van to shops and houses in the town.

Below   The survival of retailing in small towns and villages is helped where there are specialist shops. The visitor comes out of interest and ends up buying the day's groceries. Since the eighteenth century Derbyshire folk have made a living out of producing and selling ornaments made from the minerals and decorative stones from its mines, quarries and caverns. This shop in Castleton specializes in Blue-John jewellery.

Surprisingly, the majority of buildings with traditional shop fronts have had those fronts inserted, usually when the ground floor of a house has become a shop. Generally it was done so well that it is difficult to imagine the buildings not looking like that from the outset.

Prior to the architectural experimentation of this century there existed a commonly agreed building vocabulary, or kit of parts, for shop fronts which more or less guaranteed a harmonious result (see p. 112). The 'kit' consists of cornice (top projecting part), frieze or fascia (the band beneath), on which the shop's name is usually painted, pilasters (the flat columns which frame the glazed opening) and stall-riser (the panel beneath the glazed opening).

Apart from the stall-riser, the origin of which is explained by its name, they all have their origins in the classical temple. There are various secondary elements which were exploited to give architectural panache.

Above left The console bracket which supports the cornice of the baker's shop front at Eckington (see p. 112) is decorated with a stylish swag.

Above right The pilasters of a glazier's shop front, also at Eckington, are capped with consoles carved in the shape of the classical acanthus leaf motif.

Left At Ashbourne the display window of the local newspaper (known affectionately as the 'Ashbourne Stunner') has giant console brackets, which joyously defy all classical rules of proportion and scale.

To make such elaborate architectural embellishments today would be unacceptably expensive, so it makes very good economic sense to prize them and give them the care they need for their preservation.

Like chemists and pharmacists, jewellers and watchmakers often went to town on their shopfronts. This handsome example at Swadlincote was made for Henry Bowden Dinnis, the grandfather of the present shopkeeper David Dinnis who runs the business with his son Simon, a trained gemologist. H.B. Dinnis was an optician who became a pawnbroker and jeweller. The splendid lamp over the doorway, now converted to electricity, still has its gas tap. The curved glass window reveals, flanking the entrance, must have been something of a status symbol when the shop front was installed. Note the flamboyant art nouveau heads to the very slim mullions.

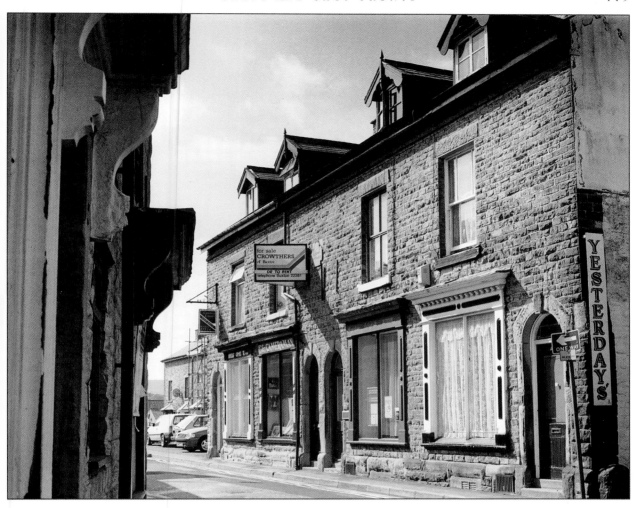

After a period of 50 years or so, during which traditional shop fronts were thought of as old-fashioned and therefore bad for trade, and hundreds were torn out or spoilt by being modernized, shopkeepers have come to realize that it is futile to compete with the big corporate stores and out-of-town shopping centres on their terms. The best route to survival and prosperity is to capitalize on the distinctive character of their businesses and, if they are fortunate enough to have them, their architecturally distinctive premises.

This group of shops in Market Street, Buxton, has survived the period of destruction virtually intact. Their appearance is made the most of with stylish signwriting and eye-catching colour schemes.

THE STREET
SCENE

While we may think of the street scene as being made up of what is seen within an urban thoroughfare, the principal factor that determines character is the historic reason for the origin of the place. For example, a medieval market town is likely to have a network of narrow routes around a wider principal street with yards branching off it which allowed further development once frontages were fully built up. An agricultural community, by contrast, will be more loosely developed with spacious gaps between farmhouses and barns. A pit village will have long terraces lining streets laid out in regular grids. This all provides the context which is then furnished with the paraphernalia of urban life.

We call lamp-posts, bus shelters, seats and bollards 'street furniture' because they furnish our public living rooms – the streets, squares, ginnels, jitties, twitchells and causeys of our towns and villages.

As with signs and nameplates, study of them can often reveal how the places in which they stand grew up and the ways of life of former inhabitants.

Unlike 'catalogue order' bollards and planters that are too often scattered randomly around newly pedestrianized streets, elements in the traditional street scene had a specific purpose and were often unique to that place.

The obelisk is a striking architectural form, used in the eighteenth century to provide a point of drama and emphasis within landscaped parks. It is used here in Matlock Bath to announce the entrance to the road leading up to The Temple, a select hotel where the Georgian visitor could get away from the hurly-burly of The Parades. The name of the hotel was clearly chosen to give connotations of the refinements of the classical world, which was further reinforced by the name of the first proprietor, Mr Aeneas Evans. It does not take much imagination to visualize the guests swishing past it in their crinolines under parasols.

This short obelisk in Matlock Bath higher up the hillside is the only other one to survive in the village, but early Victorian prints show that others once surmounted door porticos along South Parade. Their purpose was to advertise the wares of the 'museums' which sold ornaments crafted from Derbyshire minerals, including obelisks carved from black marble and Blue-John, the much prized ornamental fluorspar mined in the caverns beneath Castleton.

A more prosaic urban form is the bollard or stoop. At the entrance to Arkwright's Cromford Mill a solitary cannon-type bollard stands witness to the once near-continuous procession of goods and workers which passed in and out of the mill yard, necessitating a means of keeping cartwheels away from those on foot. It may have had a twin on the other side of the entrance. An archaeological dig has revealed the footings of a small circular building just within the mill yard, which was probably a control point for goods and workers entering and leaving the mill complex.

Opposite the mill, on the other side of the road, the need was to prevent accidental plunges into the mill leat. The numerals 182 can just be made out in the stone post, but the last numeral of the date is obliterated. Further along, the posts are of cruciform section cast iron.

When the Town Hall fronting Norfolk Square, Glossop, was developed in 1838 the square was left a rough patch of ground. It was not until later that the need for a perimeter route led to the erection of massive cast-iron bollards, possibly cast in the local foundry in George Street, which was established in 1856. The chains came even later. Recent repaving works have revealed that the stones which form the plinth for the bollards have mouldings on their undersides, indicating that they were salvaged material.

Top left   Bollards come in all shapes and sizes and perform various functions. These bulbous-topped ones in Melbourne keep a footpath exclusively for pedestrian use.

Top right and lower left   These perform the same job, as they guard entrances to the churchyards at Wirksworth (top right) and Bakewell. In Bakewell they are finely shaped from local gritstone. In Wirksworth the cast-iron stoop stands between a gritstone bollard and one of the handsome stone piers to the lych-gates of 1721.

Lower right   On occasion their purpose is no longer easily apparent. The removal of much of Buxton's railway complex has left this bollard in Station Road stranded. However, the date, 1864, cast on it neatly fixes it in time. The London & North Western and the Midland railway companies each opened their lines to Buxton on the same day – Saturday, 30 May 1863.

Above Derbyshire is not a flat county and handrails can be a welcome sight. Here, one offers help to those on the pathway on Snape Hill, Dronfield, at the foot of which stood one of the town's foundries, the works of Edward Lucas and Son Ltd, which was established beside the River Drone in 1790. Castings were produced there until 1971. It is quite possible that the posts for the handrail were made in the town.

Left A *hand*rail at The Rutland Hotel, Bakewell.

Because the ground of Derbyshire yielded up iron ore, the county had a sizeable iron industry early on. By 1806, eleven furnaces were in operation producing 10,329 tons of pig iron a year. These production figures were exceeded only by Yorkshire, Staffordshire and Shropshire. By the end of the nineteenth century, many towns had their own ironworks making a variety of goods, which often proudly bore the name of the foundry or town in raised lettering – even on the most mundane product.

At first, furnaces were fuelled by charcoal, but Abraham Darby pioneered a revolutionary technical innovation at Coalbrookdale in Shropshire by adapting a charcoal furnace to smelt iron ore with coke. Coal was readily available in Derbyshire and the coincidence of the availability of the two materials down the eastern side of the county gave the area a considerable economic advantage. Side by side with advances in furnace technology marched advances in casting methods, allowing larger and more complex items or components to be made.

The railings around the churchyard of St James, Riddings, built in 1832, are almost certainly an early product of the Oakes foundry established in 1802, which stood just down the road from the church. They are a good illustration of the complexity of casting which was being achieved by that date and show how the new material came to be used for decorative as well as purely utilitarian purposes. Even in their present rather decrepit state they speak of the charm of Georgian Gothic design.

The Georgian period spanned a range of metalworking from the classical smithying of Robert Bakewell to the advent of cast iron, and the railings to houses and churchyards from that period which adorn our towns are invariably an ornament to the street scene.

The railings outside West End House in Wirksworth are of the middle phase, in the style of Bakewell's successors, the Yates family (see p. 84). The length seen here is a masterly restoration of 1991 by local smith Simon Vaughan, filling the gap left when most of the original railings were taken for the war effort. Although severely simple, their charm lies in the way the square bar is beaten to a spear top, above the rail.

Similar railings are to be found outside The Mansion in Church Street, Ashbourne, although they are slightly more elaborate, having curled parts either side of the spearhead, making a fleur-de-lis shape. They have been attributed to Benjamin Yates. When Dr Johnson was a guest at the house, in 1777, he recorded: 'Doctor Taylor has put up a very elegant iron palisade before his house.'

The Georgian street scene was characterized by simple, uninterrupted thoroughfares, their rather stark emptiness relieved only by the occasional village pump, or the gates and railings to a grand house. Local government was limited to the activities of the magistrates and turnpike trusts, who did their best to ensure that public roads and bridges remained in reasonable order.

The new industrial age of the nineteenth century saw the emergence of a more structured form of local government, firstly run by the local vestry and then by local boards, which were driven by a desire for improvements in hygiene and seemliness. Sewers were laid, water supplies were piped, roads were metalled, causeys were paved and streets began to be lit – by gas. By the turn of the century the discovery of electricity could be taken advantage of to illuminate the newly ordered street scene.

Buxton was supplied with electricity in 1900. Between 1901 and 1902, these magnificent 'arc-lights' were erected in the town centre. They are some of the earliest electric streetlights in the country. They bear not just the name of the town but also a crest, which was designed by Robert Rippon Duke, a local architect and builder, for the Palace Hotel of 1868. It was later adopted by the local board. Around the depiction of a buck on a rock (buck-stone) is the motto *Buxtona quae calidae celebrabere nomine lymphae*, which must mean 'Buxton whose warm springs have been celebrated by fame'.

The boldness of the castings for the bridge of 1911, which carried Derby Road over the Erewash Canal at Long Eaton, is positively majestic in its scale and severity. Its abutments incorporated the supports of an earlier bridge, of 1883, which had included the abutments of the original bridge built following the construction of the canal, which began in 1777.

The magnificent chimney of Bridge Mills, of 1903, with its massive bulbous cast-iron cap, dominates the scene, giving the townscape great distinction.

Although called mills, these great industrial buildings are in fact tenement factories designed to accommodate large ace machines. Each 'mill' shared a common source of steam power but housed a number of relatively small usinesses (see pp. 73 and 74).

The quality and distinctiveness of the street scene can rest quite as much with the apparently humdrum as with the spectacular. In Long Row, Belper, the low gritstone walls which bound a gap in the terraced housing may seem nothing special, but a peep over the wall reveals that it is part of a massive railway cutting which runs through the centre of the town – one of a series of ten bridges designed by George and Robert Stephenson for their Derby to Rotherham line of 1839. The quality of the massive battered retaining walls is very fine, with a great rounded projecting band course running through the whole series. It is a purely decorative feature, but one which gives the walls great architectural character.

The brown, salt-glazed, bull-nosed brick copings in Church Street, Swadlincote, might not demand a second glance, but they help to make Swadlincote what it is – a gritty pottery town with particular traditions and a particular way of life. Around and about can be found various, and curious, manifestations of that way of life: walls made of 'dross bricks' (bricks salvaged from kilns having a rough salt-glazed surface on one side), or paving made from 'holy-boys' (floor bricks salvaged from down draught kilns), and field boundaries made of stacked salt-glazed conduit pipes which, at a casual glance, could be mistaken for hedges.

At the foot of Bolsover Castle lies the model colliery village of New Bolsover (see p. 70). Its allotments are an alternat
world – devoted to pigeon fancying as much as vegetable gardening. This is the pigeon loft of the Rodda brothers who h
had a plot since 1963 and now look after sixty-five birds.

DERBYSHIRE TERMS

Back-side The back of a house. Service road behind a row of houses

Bar A horse-way up a steep hill

Balk Hayloft

*****Banker** Mason's bench

Bawk or Balk Bressummer. Supporting timber beam or lintel

Bay Part of a barn in which corn or straw is stored

*****Black powder** Gunpowder used in quarrying. See pp. 16–19

Boskin Wooden partition in a cow house to which cows are fastened by means of an iron ring

Brag Large nail used in fastening flakes (hurdles) in fences

Brig Bridge

Brow Hill

Bulk Wooden covering over cellar steps

Byset Hollow or gutter across a road

*****Causey** Pavement. From the middle English 'causee'. See p. 106

*****Channel** Narrow passage between houses

Clamming house (clem shop) Place where beast is put for night to empty itself before it is slaughtered

Clap post Post against which a field gate closes

Cloose (Close) Field

Clough Valley

Cock loft Ordinary upper room, mostly in the roof. Garret

Dagging can Watering can

*****Delf** Stone quarry

Dike Brook or rivulet

Dot'ill Spoil heap

*****Down spout** Drainpipe. Rainwater pipe. See p. 50

*****Eel post** Post on which a field gate is hung

Easing Eaves. House-easing

*****Entry** Narrow passage or tunnel between houses (snicket further north). See also tunnel entry

Ewsing Eaves of a house

*****Feathers** Metal wedges. Used for splitting stone in a quarry. See p. 18

*****Footrill** Inclined passage or tunnel by which coal or other mineral is obtained

Fore-tree Piece of wood to keep up the bedding in a cow house

Fotherom Fodder-room. Small place behind the fodder rack

Fould Farmyard

*****Fox-earth** Brown (red) earth

---

* terms known to be still in use

*Gate Road, the street or way. From the Old Norse 'gata'

*Gennel/Ginnel Entry or narrow passage between two houses. Passage inside a cow house. Steps down between coal houses into a backyard

Gimmers Hinges

*Goit/Goyt Floodgate. Waterchannel

Groop Drain behind the cows in a cow house

Ground-sill Threshold

*House/House Place Living room. Kitchen of a cottage

Hud/Hool/Hood Hob of a fireplace

Hull Any small covered building, e.g. pen or coop

*Jawm (Jamb) Post of a door or window

*Jitty Passage between buildings or boundary walls. Small lane

Kirk Church

*Kibble Small tub for drawing water out of a well

*Lander Long wooden trough to convey water over a distance

*Lat Lath for plastering

Lathe Barn

*Launder Spout. Channel for water. Roof guttering

Miln Mill

Pane-drawn Plastered between spars (rafters) only

Pank-aase Water closet, outside toilet

Parge To lay on the first coat in plastering. To plaster inside flue or chimney

Pig-coit Pig-sty

Pig hull Pig-sty

Pleaching Layering a hedge

*Plug Long chisel. Used for splitting stone in a quarry. See p. 18

*Raddle Red earth used to mark sheep and colour limewash

Rig tree Highest beam in the roof of a house

Riggin Ridge of a house

Riggin stones Topmost stones of the ridge on a roof

*Scutch Mason's tool

Sell Sill of a door

*Sets/Setts Stone paving units. Edge stones which divide a footpath from the road. See p. 107

Shippon Cow house

Sill Threshold

Sneck Latch of a door. Wooden latch

*Sough Drain or adit to de-water a mine. Domestic drain

*Spouting Rainwater downpipe. Roof guttering. See p. 45

*Spar Pole. Rafter

Sparrow Short nail with a broad, thick head

Spot A place – henspot, pig spot, etc

Stack-broach Thatch peg

Stele Stile

Stiff Ladder

*Stoop Post fastened in the earth. Bollard. See pp. 83 and 124

Thak Thatch

Thak-peggs Hazel or elder bands used to fasten down straw covering a haystack

*Thrall Stone shelf in a pantry or cellar

*Toach/(torch) To seal the underside of roof slates or tiles with lime-hair plaster

*Torr Hill, large rock

*Trows Roof guttering. See p. 47

Tub Coal wagon

*Tunnel entrance Passage through building to yard behind. See p. 109

*Twitchel Passage between buildings or boundary walls

Vennel Secondary track or path

Wild worm pattern An ornamentation of the walls of bedrooms

Win A common, e.g. Hognaston Win, where gorse or furze grows

Yate Gate

USEFUL ADDRESSES

For advice on the care and maintenance of historic buildings and historic areas, the nearest source is the conservation officer of the local planning authority. The names and addresses of the local authorities for Derbyshire are:

*Amber Valley Borough Council,
P O Box 18,
Town Hall,
Market Place,
Ripley DE5 3SZ.
Tel: 01773 570 222.

*Bolsover District Council,
Sherwood Lodge,
Bolsover,
Chesterfield S44 6NF.
Tel: 01246 240 000.

Chesterfield Borough Council,
Town Hall,
Chesterfield S40 1LP.
Tel: 01246 345 345.

*Derby City Council,
Roman House,
Friargate,
Derby DE1 1XB.
Tel: 01332 255 901.

Derbyshire Dales District Council,
Town Hall,
Matlock DE4 3NN.
Tel: 01629 580 580.

Erewash Borough Council,
Town Hall,
Long Eaton,
NG10 1HU.
Tel: 0115 9461 321.

*High Peak Borough Council,
Municipal Buildings,
Glossop SK13 8AF.
Tel: 01457 851 600.

*North East Derbyshire District Council,
Council House,
Saltergate,
Chesterfield S40 1LF.
Tel: 01246 231 111.

*South Derbyshire District Council,
Civic Offices,
Civic Way,
Swadlincote,
DE11 0AH.
Tel: 01283 221 000.

* Councils with conservation officers.

In addition, Derbyshire County Council has a Conservation and Design team which provides expert advice on archaeology, conservation areas, historic buildings, historic gardens, historic landscapes and design matters.

The team maintains a register of building crafts people and sources of traditional building materials and artefacts. Enquiries can be made by telephone on 01629 580 000 exts 7182, 7183 and 7184. The team also maintains a list of historic buildings in Derbyshire which are considered to be at risk by virtue of disrepair, disuse or unsympathetic use. Although most of the buildings on the list are not for sale in the normal sense, enquiries from persons wishing to purchase a historic building in order to repair it and bring it into use are welcomed.

LOCAL AMENITY SOCIETIES AND VOLUNTARY GROUPS CONCERNED WITH THE BUILT ENVIRONMENT

There are more than fifty voluntary groups in Derbyshire committed to the protection and enhancement of the built environment. Derbyshire County Council publishes and maintains a list of these groups, with details of names and addresses of contacts.

NATIONAL AMENITY SOCIETIES AND OTHER CONSERVATION BODIES

The Society for the Protection of Ancient Buildings (SPAB), 37 Spital Square, London E1 6DY. Tel: 0171 377 1644.

This was the first of the national amenity societies, founded by William Morris in 1877. It concentrates on cases relating to pre-1700 buildings, and produces a comprehensive set of technical pamphlets and information sheets on the repair of historic buildings.

The Ancient Monuments Society, St Ann's Vestry Hall, 2 Church Entry, London EC4V 5HB. Tel: 0171 236 3934.

Founded in 1924 in Manchester, this organization places great emphasis on the study of historic buildings, and to support this it publishes its well respected annual *Transactions*. There is a working partnership with the Friends of Friendless Churches, which owns 20 disused but historically important churches in England and Wales.

The Georgian Group, 6 Fitzroy Square, London W1P 6DX.
Tel: 0171 387 1720.

The Georgian Group works for an increased understanding and appreciation of Georgian and Regency architecture and, like the other societies, has published practical guides for owners. Besides application casework, its principal activity is organizing visits to Georgian buildings and sites.

The Victorian Society, 1 Priory Gardens, Bedford Park, London W4 1TT.
Tel: 0181 994 1019.

The Northern Casework Office (which covers Derbyshire) is Cornmill Cottage, Water Lane, Cranford. DE4 3QH.
Tel: 01629 826837

The Victorian Society was formed, in 1958, in response to the apparent lack of public appreciation of Victorian architecture. Visits to Victorian buildings are arranged, and the Society produces guides for owners of Victorian buildings. Part of its specialist role is to comment on applications affecting listed buildings of the Victorian period.

The Council for British Archaeology, Bowes Morrell House, 111 Walmgate, York YO1 9WA.
Tel: 01904 671 417.

The Council for British Archaeology exists to promote the study and safegaurding of Britain's historic environment, to provide a forum for archaelogical opinion and to improve public knowledge of Britain's past.

Council for the Protection of Rural England (CPRE), Warwick House, 25 Buckingham Palace Road, London SW1W 0PP.
Tel: 0171 976 6433.

This is a very active campaign organization, based on local branches and sub-branches. The CPRE is generally less involved with buildings in detail, but is much concerned with the strategic view and with changes to the countryside. The contact names and addresses of the branches covering Derbyshire are given in the County Council's list of local amenity societies.

The Civic Trust, 17 Carlton House Terrace, London SW1Y 5AW.
Tel: 0171 930 0914.

A trust formed especially to promote the improvement of towns and cities, and the body to which many local civic societies are affiliated.

SAVE Britain's Heritage, 70 Cowcross St, London EC1M 6EJ.
Tel: 0171 253 3500.

This conservation pressure group runs campaigns to oppose demolition or neglect of some of the more important historic buildings and categories of buildings. It also publishes a very useful report, *Buildings at Risk*, mostly compiled from information sent in by local councils.

Common Ground, PO Box 25309, London NW5 1ZA.
Tel: 0171 267 2144.

A small campaigning organization committed to raising environmental awareness through innovative model projects, exhibitions, publications and events. One of its model projects is a campaign for local distinctiveness.

ENGLISH HERITAGE AND GOVERNMENT CONSERVATION AGENCIES

English Heritage, East Midlands Team, Conservation Group, 23 Savile Row, London W1X 1AB.
Tel: 0171 973 3000.

English Heritage was created by the Government in 1984 to take over all of the building conservation duties formerly carried out by the Department of the Environment. The area teams deal with proposals affecting the higher grades of listed buildings but can also be a useful source of specialist advice. If grant aid from English Heritage is to be discussed, this should be done through the area team. Initially, however, contact should be made with the conservation officer of the local council.

Department of Culture, Media & Sport, Heritage Division, Third Floor, 2–4 Cockspur Street, London SW1Y 5DH.
Tel: 0171 211 6000.

After the creation of English Heritage, some legal functions continued to be administered by the Department of the Environment. In 1992 the Government created a new department which would deal with such matters as the listing of buildings, approval for compulsory purchase of listed buildings and other legal matters. Request for additions to the statutory list should be made to the above address. The County Council's Heritage & Design team can give advice about how best to present such a request.

Royal Commission on the Historical Monuments of England, NMRC, Kemble Drive, Swindon SN2 2GZ.
Tel: 01793 414 600.

This standing Royal Commission was created in 1908 to provide a record of archaeology and buildings in England. The commission has one of the largest collections of photographs of buildings in the country, housed in parish-by-parish box files held in the National Buildings Record. These are available for public inspection.

There is a further statutory role for the commission in that applications affecting the historic structure of listed buildings must be notified to the Commission so that they can decide whether the building merits recording, by photographs, a report or a drawn record. The regional office which deals with this aspect of the commission's work is Shelley House, Acomb Road, York YO2 4HB. Tel: 01904 784 411.

Torr Vale Mill and its weir in the gorge of the River Goyt at New Mills. Of several mills which operated in the gorge (known as The Torrs) it is the only one to remain in use, for cotton spinning.

FURTHER READING

GENERAL BACKGROUND

Clifford, Sue and King, Angela (eds). *Local Distinctiveness: Place, Particularity and Identity, Essays for a Conference*, Common Ground Publications, 1993. A wide-ranging number of viewpoints on local identity. A campaign document.

Clifton-Taylor, Alec. *The Pattern of English Building*, 4th edn, Faber, 1987. A comprehensive picture of building traditions based on the materials used and the way they relate to geology, geography and historical background. A classic.

McGhie, Caroline and Girling, Richard. *Local Attraction: the Design of New Housing in the Countryside*, Council for the Preservation of Rural England, 1995. A plea for high standards of design for new houses and a commitment to respecting local distinctiveness. A campaign document.

DERBYSHIRE STUDIES

Farey, John. *General View of the Agriculture and Minerals of Derbyshire*, B McMillan, Vol. I 1811, Vol. II 1813. Immensely detailed survey. Vol. I covers geology, mineral and stone production; Vol. II includes building styles, methods and materials. A remarkable picture of Georgian Derbyshire.

Thorold, Henry. *Derbyshire: a Shell Guide*, Faber, 1972. Well illustrated gazetteer with a short, but very informative, introductory overview of the county, its history, geography and architecture. Still the best county guide.

CARE OF BUILDINGS

Lander, Hugh. *The House Restorer's Guide*, David & Charles, 1986 and 1992. Practical guidance to understanding and caring for traditional buildings.

Saunders, Matthew. *The Historic Home Owner's Companion*, Batsford 1987 – Advice addressed to owners of historic buildings. Deals with law, history, construction and aesthetics.

Advisory booklets on the history and methods of repair of various architectural elements, for example doors, windows, brickwork, stonework and cast iron, are available from the Society for the Protection of Ancient Buildings, The Georgian Group and The Victorian Society (see p. 140).

GLOSSARIES

Addy, Sidney Oldall. *A Glossary of Words used in the Neighbourhood of Sheffield*, English Dialect Society, 1888. The classic on the subject for northern Derbyshire.

Addy also wrote two supplements of additional terms. Addy, Sidney Oldall. 'Local words and their meanings' *Trans. Hunter Arch. Soc.* 4(2), 1931–2.

Pegg, Samuel. *Two Collections of Derbicisms*, English Dialect Society, 1896. Complementary but independent research, also covering the north-east Derbyshire area.

Scollins, Richard and Titford, John. *Ey Up Mi Duck*, Ilkeston, published privately, Pt 1 1976, Pt 2 1976, Pt 3 1977. Light-hearted but well-researched studies of the dialect of the twentieth-century Ilkeston and Erewash Valley area with substantial glossaries.

INDEX OF PLACES

ACKNOWLEDGEMENTS

The authors thank all those who assisted in the preparation of this book. In addition to those people named, particular thanks are due to property owners, some of whom appear in the pages, and to those who facilitated the chapter on building crafts. Special thanks are also due to members of the voluntary groups listed below for nominating suggestions for images to be included:

The Arkwright Society, Bakewell Civic Society, Belper Historical Society, Bolsover Civic Society, Buxton Civic Society, Chesterfield Civic Society, Dronfield Civic Society, Old Dronfield Society, Eckington Civic Society, Glossop Heritage Centre, Ilkeston Civic Society, Matlock Civic Society, Melbourne Civic Society, Midlands Amenity Societies Association, New Mills Heritage Centre, Peak District Mines Historical Society, Renishaw Local History Society and Wirksworth Civic Society.

Mr W. Bailey, Mr A. Blacklay, Mr J. Brighton, Mr D. Brumhead, Dr C. Charlton, Mrs M. Davies, Ms D. Dorrell, Mr M. Doughty, Revd J. Drackley, Mr A. Edwards, Mr P. Gibbons, Ms B. Haigh, Ms M. Hallard, Mrs Handford, Mr M. Handley, Mr R. Hawkins, Mr P. Heath, Mr A. Henstock, Mrs W. Hope, Mr B. Howitt, Mrs J. Jenkinson, Mr M. Jobling, Mr J. Leech, Mr I. McKay, Mr C. Margerrison, Mr C. Maskery, Mrs D. Mason, Mr D. Mellor, Ms J. Michell, Mr R. Nixon, Mr N. Overton, Mr J. Pearson, Mr R. Pearson, Mrs J. Radford, Mr K. Reedman, Mr E. Saunders, Mr A. Sebire, Mr J. Storer, Dr P. Strange, Mr I. Thomas, Mr R. Tuffrey, Mr S. and Mrs J. Vaughan.

Thanks are also due to Paul Adam of The Dark Room for his printing of the black-and-white images and to Propix for the colour images.

Finally, particular thanks are due to the long-suffering wives of the three authors.